Derek Press

Printed by Derek Press, Cleveland, Tennessee

Sources:

King James Version Bible
Center For Food Safety (Monsanto vs. U.S. Farmers)
Southeast Farm Press
Seed Today
U.S.D.A.
The Huntsville Times
LINK TV
Science Daily
Webster's Dictionary
Joe Camden "The Terminator Gene"
Monsanto
ETC Group
Francis Bacon
Source Watch
Fine Arts Collection
David Jeremiah
Helen Blavatsky
Texe Marrs
Wayne Murphee, Photography
Auther S. Maxwell

ISBN: 978-1-59684-351-6

Whitehorse LLC. • 132 Peachtree Street
Scottsboro, Alabama 35768
www.whitehorsellc.com
E-mail: whitehorsellc@centurytel.net

Printed by Derek Press, Cleveland, TN

CONTENTS

DEDICATION

I dedicate this book to all who read it and gain spiritual understanding from it. You are of the utmost importance to me even though we may never meet in this world. To the many people who have supported me in prayer the last few years. To my daughters, Valerie and Emily who have suffered greatly during this ordeal. To my father who did not understand how he could be sued for something he did not do. To Don Word, my first attorney, who has been a friend to the end. To my brilliant patent attorneys in Huntsville, Alabama. To people in high places who did not have to help me but chose to. To God Almighty, the creator of seed, for giving me guidance and inspiration to write this book.

—Michael White

FOREWORD

Simple things can at times become the most profound. Look at small grains of seed. Seed comes in all sizes, shapes, and colors. The end purpose of all, however, is to reproduce. Most of us have had the experience of putting seed into the ground and watching with wonder as the earth produces a bounty. It has been customary for generations for a part of that harvest to be saved back, for the start of next year's crops. This scenario constantly repeated, has marked the pages of our past history. At one time over ninety percent of our population was involved in farming, so I am told. Seed and food are intertwined to support human life. Seed, rich soil and hard working people has been the combination that our heavenly Father has used to build our great nation.

Could such a simple process, one that actually undergirds our lives, our very civilization be changed? This seems to be a natural, God-given process that is fully ingrained in our way of life. Food is life and to have food one must have seed. Seed may look simple, but they are deeply profound!

What would happen if some individual or some Corporation gained control over our food supply? Control of any product carries with it a certain amount of power. The more important a product is, the more power that control would bring. Is there any product more important than our food? He who controls our seed supply controls our food supply. Joseph did it in Egypt. Many dictators have done it throughout history. "We are what we eat", is an adage we hear often. "An army marches on it's stomach", is another common one. A powerful control over any people is the control of their food supply.

Michael White, the author of this book, believes there is an attempt being made by a global corporation to gain control of our seed supply. He details many events from his own experience and many other farmers in the United States. Facts and figures are given that should cause you to pause and reflect on what is happening here in the land of the free! With food prices rising and so many farmers leaving or being forced out of the business, someone needs to become concerned of the plight with the farmer.

I have known Michael since he was a small boy. He is a boyhood friend of my own son. I was his pastor for possibly thirty years. He is a dedicated Christian. He has been a farmer all of his life as was his father before him. He has worked hard and shown that independent entrepreneurial spirit that is prevalent in so many American farmers. You will read how he fought to maintain that good life he had built.

You will read in this book how our farmers are harassed and strangled as they try to continue to feed us. You will also be made aware of the difficulty which they face as they, with limited resources, try to fight back against ruthless regulations which favor the huge corporations. With seemingly unlimited funds, compared to individual farmers, these groups of high powered lawyers and corporations grasp for more control and more power each year. Are our courts and judges asleep? How can corporations dodge those time honored, landmark decisions such as the Sherman Anti-trust Act and others like it? Who is big enough to challenge them? "Is there no balm in Gilead?"

Michael White also sees another factor entering this conflict. He is a deeply spiritual man and is a student of Bible Prophecy. He believes sincerely that the "Man of Sin", that charismatic strong man of Daniel and Revelation, will come one day with his one world rule and government. His trump cards will not only include false religion and great military power but will also include the control of food hence the control of seed!

Is the head of that dragon appearing? (Revelation 13:17)

Read this book carefully and prayerfully before you make your decision. As author Francis Bacon said, "this book must be digested ."

Romans 13:11 *And that, knowing the time that now it is high time to wake out of sleep......*

God bless the American farmer.

Rev, Richard L. Tyler, Jr.
Ordained Bishop
Church of God

Introduction

The 666's Are in the Seed

Revelation 13:18 {KJV} Here is ***wisdom***. Let him that hath understanding count the number of the beast: for it is the number of a man; and his number is Six hundred threescore and six.

As you begin reading this book, pray for understanding, discernment, and **wisdom**. This is the first book I have ever written and writing it actually shocks me because I do not consider or proclaim myself to be a writer.

This book contains parts of my fifty years of life. The main focus is on the last four years of my life. Please do not prematurely draw the conclusion that I am writing solely about myself. This book's center of attention is to be directed entirely toward a four-letter word which is "**SEED**."

I believe seed to be the one most essential item that is necessary to give and maintain all forms of life. The most important form of life is human life. I invite you into my life so that you may better understand the importance of seed.

The type of seed that I will mainly focus on is agricultural seed. Without the agricultural seed, this world would immediately be thrust into starvation and unmeasurable loss of life.

Concentrate slowly as we walk through a secretive factual door that leads into a room that you probably do not know exists. In this room the secret of patented seed lies unnoticed by the majority of the general public. I believe that this patented seed is now being used to plant more than 90 percent of America's farm land. It is also covering the world and is very active in the World Trade Order (WTO).

Hundreds of farmers have either been sued or have been threatened with lawsuits for saving their own seed. My 82-year-old father and I are only two of these countless farmers that are in lawsuits. We were sued in 2003 for saving seed, selling seed, and cleaning seed by a company called Monsanto. The lawsuit which is still pending in Federal Court has caused much pain and suffering to be inflicted upon me and my family in a manner which is hard to measure. My wife, Debbie, of twenty-two years and I have gone through a very heartbreaking divorce. My daughters, Valerie, age 21, and Emily, age eight, can no longer be called an intact family. My father, who stopped farming around 1970, does not understand and has been devastated by this lawsuit. I had to close my twenty-one year-old seed business down because Monsanto stalked most of my customers and threatened them with lawsuits.

We buried my mother in 2004 during this ordeal. She was a Christian for more than sixty years, attending church close to 12,000 times. I am at peace that she is now in perfect happiness abiding in her destiny. Due to her health conditions, she knew very little about the lawsuit. My father, my family, and I will continue to suffer for quite sometime. The trial is expected to take place in Huntsville, Alabama's Federal Court in the late summer of 2006. It is a civil lawsuit, not a criminal lawsuit.

In April 2004 my health deteriorated from depression and fear and several months of no appetite. I lost so much weight that my body and mind quit working, and I had a nervous breakdown. I ended up in a Birmingham, Alabama, hospital under the care of a doctor by the name of William Howell. It just so happened that he was well aware of Monsanto's evil side. Monsanto and affiliate, Solutia, were defendants in a major lawsuit in Anniston, Alabama, where they were accused of illegally dumping toxic chemicals. Around 2002, Monsanto and Solutia reached a court settlement after the suit had been going on for several years. Dr. Howell told me he was one of the lead doctors representing the people of Anniston.

Monsanto's iniquity had preceded me even to my hospital bed and doctors. I believe that this is the last doctor in the world that Monsanto would have wanted me to be under the care of. God has restored my health and sanity and given me an arsenal of ammunition to fight this giant with. The pain and suffering that I have experienced has strengthened me for the battle that is still to come.

God gave us seed in Genesis 1:11, and Monsanto has taken the liberty to genetically modify and patent them. Monsanto does not sell seed, they sell patented technology, which gives them control of seed. I feel that I have already lost everything on this earth that has ever meant anything to me except for God and the periodic time that I get to spend with my children and my church family. One thing that I did lose which was a beneficial loss was the spirit of fear. I no longer have any fear of Monsanto in the courtroom because I believe God wants this court case to take place. God does not want the take-over of HIS seed to go unnoticed. God does not want the Christian world or the sinner world to have this biblical secret hidden from them. To own and control His seed gives the owner a hidden control over all forms of life. God has told me that this seed control will give the anti-Christ his greatest weapon to govern this world. The court proceedings whatever the outcome, will give me the knowledge to write this book.

I do not feel worthy to untie the shoes of any of the people that God used in the Holy Bible. I would not write this book if I had a choice, but I have no choice. God has told me to write and tell you that "*The **666's** are in the seed.*"

By Michael White

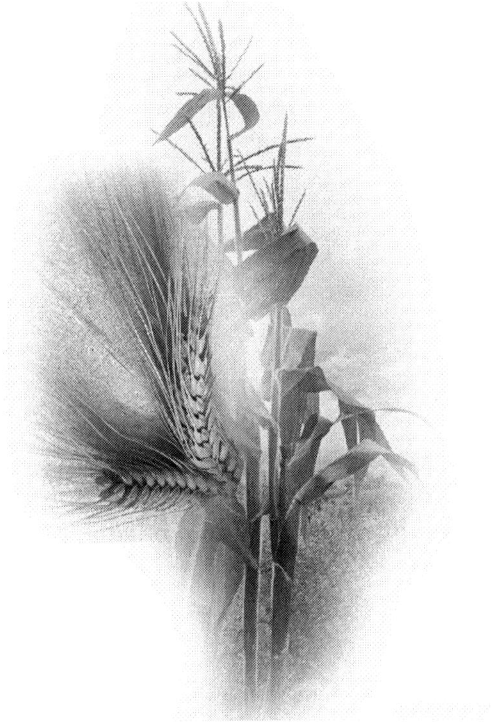

1 Be A Good Steward

The word "steward" has a dictionary definition of "a person as being a caretaker of land or food." It is no accident that Monsanto calls their worldwide seed guide manual *The Monsanto Technology Agreement*.

There are other seed guides written by other large seed companies that are similar to Monsanto's. It seems all of these guides boast of themselves and tell farmers the great things they are doing for farmers and the world. However, they fail to tell you of their ultimate goal, which is to own and control the world seed supply. I'm constantly reminded as I visit farm supply stores by things people say. I have recently listened to people ask for seed to plant in their gardens and they are being told that many types of old varieties of seed are not available anymore. Most of the time these are elderly people and I watch their facial expressions when they just simply cannot believe they can no longer buy certain seed that have been around for decades or perhaps hundreds or thousands of years.

Although these major seed companies are competitors, they join ranks to gain control of seed. Other seed companies using Monsanto's technology causes farmers to adhere to Monsanto's stewardship program if they purchase seed from their company, even though Monsanto does not own their company. Monsanto's technology is being integrated into almost all of the largest seed companies.

Many seed companies are taking the smallest pack of garden seed and telling you that you cannot save seed from what this small packet produces. Some of these small packets say "protected variety" or "restricted use" which often means you can't save seed from them. The noose is now tightened on seed to the extent that if a genetically modified or patented seed falls from a truck, it would be illegal for you to plant it. I know some of you readers will find this hard to believe, but the word "any" means as little as one.

All seed guides that I have read make it illegal to save almost any type seed. The commonly used statement used by these seed guides forces you to agree to use these "for a single crop only." This has been a very effective system going from saving seed ten years ago to not being able to save hardly any now. At this rate it is inevitable that 100 percent control is in their grasp soon.

I have a friend at a major university who recently told me they had purchased a new wheat variety which is not patented, and he wants me to grow and multiply it. I intend to do so and even with this I run the risk of a few genetically modified seeds being in my fields. Nature such as birds or even farm equipment that had been used in the planting or harvesting of genetically modified crops will trans-locate seed in almost every instance. It is certainly possible for anyone who wants to entrap you to throw out genetically modified seed by hand or aircraft. It is also very likely when you buy conventional seed that those conventional seed are not 100 percent pure or free from genetically modified contamination.

I am not so naive as to think I have any chance at stopping this monster seed plan. It is fueled by tens of thousands of men such as lawyers, scientists, politicians, lobbyists, and countless others. Billions of dollars are fueling this system.

Who am I that I should attack these stewardship agreements that are fast becoming law without the majority of the world population noticing?

I have had to put my face on the floor in shame of my walk with God in my 50 years of life and say I'm not worthy to write this book. I've had to come to the realization that this book is being written with the inspiration of the Spirit of the Living God. Sometimes when I consider all that has happened, I catch myself asking myself, "Who am I?"

I've come to the understanding that my job is to expose this seed system and not try to stop it. My goal is to make you, the reader, understand the gigantic end-time biblical significance of it.

My divorce, lawsuits, the closing of my seed business, the suing of my 82-year-old father and many other issues have been very painful. As for my father, I've never fully understood why Monsanto sued him. I can still vividly remember a young man who worked for Monsanto's attorneys bringing my lawsuits to my home. After this young man gave me my lawsuit, he asked where Wayne White (my father) lived. I asked him why he wanted to know and he said he also had paperwork to deliver to him. I asked the young man if he would let me give it to him and he reluctantly agreed. When I read the paperwork and saw that my elderly father was being sued by Monsanto, my heart almost failed in disbelief. My father was already grieving over my mother's terrible health conditions. I actually didn't tell my father he was sued for about three months. I tried to spare him all the pain I could. As bad as it was, the suing of my father became the catalyst for my determination to fight Monsanto. See photo #1 in the photo section of this book, this was the condition my father and mother were in when Monsanto sued him.

I can remember the look on my father's face when I told him Monsanto was also suing him. Most people in the community could not understand how Monsanto could be so brazen to stoop so low as this. After all, most people felt they had destroyed enough lives in Anniston, Alabama, with the illegal dumping of hazardous chemicals. The earth was already planted with countless victims of agent orange, a chemical that Monsanto produced and sold.

I will briefly address the tragedy Monsanto brought upon the resident's of Anniston, Alabama. The source for this information comes from the environmental watch group SourceWatch.

In the Washington Post article (Jan 1, 2002) "Monsanto Hid Decades of Pollution PCBs Drenched Ala. Town, But No One Was Ever Told" a grim story of Monsanto's treacherous behavior in Anniston Alabama was revealed. It is summed up in this chilling paragraph: "They also know that for nearly 40 years, while producing the now-banned industrial coolants known as PCBs at a local factory, Monsanto Co. Routinely discharged toxic waste into a west Anniston creek and dumped millions of pounds of PCBs into oozing open-pit landfills. And thousands of pages of Monsanto documents- - many emblazoned with warnings such as "CONFIDENTIAL: Read and Destroy" - - show that for decades, the corporate giant concealed what it did and what it knew."

"In 1966, Monsanto managers discovered that fish submerged in that creek turned belly-up within 10 seconds, spurting blood and shedding skin as if dunked into boiling water. They told no one."

"Sylvester Harris, 63, an undertaker who lived across the street from the plant, said he always thought he was burying too many young children. 'I knew something was wrong around here,' he said."

I have recently begun to see the benefits of these battles instead of the negative effect of them. I equal them to having made several trips to the front line of a war. With the survival of each battle, I receive the strength to fight the next one even if it promises to be worse than the one before. The writing of this book has been a battle and I also expect a severe backlash from Monsanto after this book is published. I have read and heard that almost everyone who tries to write about Monsanto is threatened with a lawsuit. I am very aware that Monsanto will probably threaten me with another lawsuit if they gain knowledge of this book before I publish it. They sued my elderly father for something he didn't do, so it would be of no surprise to me to get sued for writing this book. In this situation my decision comes easy. The decision I'm talking about is for me to face Monsanto in a Federal courtroom or throw the book away and face God for not writing it. Monsanto's wrath would be a bunny rabbit compared to me standing before God and telling Him that I did not publish the book because I was afraid of what Monsanto might do.

Countless people from many arenas will attack me on this book. I believe, however, many more people will accept it than the number which choose to fight me. We are already seeing potential for millions of environmentalists and other groups being on our side instead of Monsanto's. I believe joy will come in the morning in time to spare my sanity.

The Monsanto Technology Agreement seems to be much more aggressive than other seed companies. It is my opinion that other seed companies are proud of Monsanto's aggressiveness, though they won't admit it. Monsanto is unashamed to frivolously sue such people as my elderly father while his wife, my mother, lay dying (they seem to wish to keep his lawsuit a secret). They have not even depositioned him because they are ashamed to face him in person.

I'll let Monsanto's own record prove their evilness in the poisoning of thousands of people in Anniston, Alabama. They (Monsanto/Solutia) fought the lawsuit against them and filed bankruptcy when the truth came out of the protracted court battle in Anniston of 2003. They told some of our elected officials within days after they settled that lawsuit that they were going to sue 75 Alabama farmers. Some state officials told me Monsanto said I would be the first to be sued. I was the first to get sued. I have to believe that it was no "coincidence" in the close correlation of their lawsuit in Anniston and their quick announcement they were going to sue 75 Alabama farmers.

The scary part is they lead the race in suing farmers and also lead in seed patents. A very self-proven (agent orange) evil corporation has taken control of God's first gift to humanity, which is seed.

I thank God now for their attacks on me and, believe it or not, I thank Monsanto. Their attacks have helped give me the armor and wisdom to write this book.

In all of their silencing of farmers and arbitration board slaughters, they have covered themselves by copyrighting their seed manual. I was unsure if that copyright prevented me from writing this chapter using their seed guide to expose their unbelievable practices. I'll call their seed guide book their "seed bible", but I'm unable to use it in this chapter. I am certainly not stupid enough to ask their permission to use parts of their seed guide in this book. I have attempted to keep this book a secret from them. They have safeguarded themselves in all areas, including the Federal Courts. Many farmers who have settled with them, in or out of court, have agreed to remain silent. I believe that most of these farmers are forced to buy Monsanto's seed and enter into their stewardship program after litigation. This allows Monsanto the right to enter their fields in the future to obtain samples for DNA testing. Monsanto had a court order to go into my fields. In January 2004 they brought 10 to 15 people with them, including two security guards, to test my fields for Monsanto's technology. The tests they pulled in my fields came back negative. The security guards stood at my place of business while the other people went to my fields. I requested some agricultural authorities to help monitor the situation, but they refused. However, a high ranking official at Auburn University came to my fields and helped monitor these people, that I simply did not trust. They have used many methods, legal and illegal, to enforce this seed policy.

If my accusing them of using illegal methods surprises you, please note that I have video of some of their investigators breaking laws to back-up my accusations. I believe Monsanto is aware of my videos because I aimed the camera on some of their people and I believe they probably told Monsanto or their lawyers about me using a camera on them. They took thousands of pictures of my customers and farmers in north Alabama, so I felt entitled to have the right to use a camera on them. However, Monsanto calls that counter-surveillance, and they do not like it. There was nothing illegal about it so they can just get over it.

When I first discovered their seed manual was copyrighted, my heart weakened knowing that it contained many hidden secrets that I needed to use in this book. Monsanto may not call it secrets, but when I ask farmers if they know they have agreed to control pollen flow when they sign Monsanto's agreements, the farmers laugh at me because this is impossible.

Having worried about my inability to write this chapter as it needs to be written, several months went by with this chapter on hold. I knew in my heart the importance of this chapter, and felt that it needed to be the first chapter of this book. This chapter is the best way God has given me to allow you to understand what is going on. My first lawyer told me it took him one full year to understand this "thing" and believe it was actually happening.

A few days ago my mind was shocked when I realized what had been lying at my fingertips. At my fingertips was a scrapbook given to me in 2004 by Monsanto's lawyers. It was given to me by my lawyers, having received it from the Federal Court process. This scrapbook, which I called a Christmas gift, contained pages and pages of Monsanto boasting of what they were doing to farmers. I believe they mailed it to me to add depression to my mind as I was about to go through the first Christmas of my life without my family intact. I believe this **gift** was designed to taunt me and create fear. This scrapbook actually had writings cut out with scissors and taped to a page.

In these pages they boasted of their past, present, and future success. They showed pictures of farmers being forced to destroy their own crops. Monsanto's pride, dominance, and zero compassion on anyone spilled from these pages. God grabbed my feeble mind and told me, *"Monsanto themselves had given me exactly what I needed."* I immediately met with my lawyer, we discussed their **gift** to me, and realized that they failed to copyright this **gift**, or ask for the court's protection. The gift I am talking about is a stack of photocopied paperwork that we called a scrapbook that Monsanto sent to us when we requested different documents. This scrapbook had actually angered my lawyer and he didn't want to give it to me. He had no choice because it came through the Federal Court and he had to give it to me. That's the way the court system works.

It is amazing how God can take the mistakes that the enemy makes and use it to destroy them. Listen, Monsanto lawyers who are responsible for this **gift**, grind your teeth and let your faces become blood red. I state my source for the information to write this chapter, having been given to me by you, yourselves. If it chokes you, which it will, curse yourselves. Thank you, **GOD**, for causing them to send me this much needed **gift** of information.

It is 9-11-05 as I sit in my church on Sunday morning. Our Pastor has asked us to remember the two disasters that have struck our country. The first of course was the World Trade Center attack and the other being the recent hurricane, Katrina. I will not refer much more through this book to these disasters. That is not what God has called me to do.

My calling is to write of a much more evil and terrible

time that this world has yet to endure. This book is to tell you of a time that will be so terrible that this world has never seen before nor ever shall see again.

The writing of this book is entering its third year. It has not been easy having lost my Mother, health, sanity, seed business, wife and children (because of a divorce), none of which I wanted, and many other hardships.

This book is mainly written concerning patented seed which is primarily agriculture and vegetable. This book is an attempt to give you the understanding of how important seed is. It will cause you to understand how dangerous it is for all seed to be patented and owned by a handful of companies. Understand when you hear the words "genetically modified food" or GMF, that this food has to come from genetically modified seed. You can easily compare altering seed to cloning humans and animals.

You will read at the beginning of this book without understanding, but it is my GOD-given calling to help you understand. You will have a hard time with my attack upon a large corporation by the name of Monsanto. It will be hard for you to understand how I proclaim to be a Christian and write some of the things in which I am writing. You will understand that Almighty God is with me and confirms that with His scripture.

I personally understand how hard it will be for you to believe that seed can be so important. I know it is hard to understand that seed will be the most powerful weapon a corporation or person can have to control the human race. There is no better place for me to prove the importance of seed than the scriptures themselves. I'll start your understanding with God's own actions in **Genesis 1:11** {KJV} *And God said, Let the earth bring forth grass, the herb yielding* ***seed****, and the fruit tree yielding fruit after his kind, whose* ***seed*** *is in itself, upon the earth: and it was so.* In Monsanto's scrapbook that they mailed me they showed a picture of a farmer plowing up 287 acres of soybeans.

They also boast of taking 1200 bags of soybeans from this farmer. They boast by saying he is currently undergoing legal prosecution in the court system. Understand, Monsanto is so powerful they can sue a farmer for saving seed. They can force him to destroy his crop, which God says seed are supposed to replenish and not be destroyed. Then they can force him to comply with their unbelievable agreements. They call people who save seed, seed pirates. They boast of taking huge amounts of money from farmers who save seed. I, myself, call Monsanto a pirate of God's seed.

As complex and deceptive as this world seed take-over is, it becomes simple when you look at God's reasoning when He first created seed. Understand that *as soon as God* gathered the waters together, which created dry land, that He called Earth–He had put a chain of events into motion. Some of those events were the creation of the sun, moon, stars, sea life and bird life; He then created animal life and MAN. We must understand, *God* created all of these events in sequence .

Let us put the important word **SEED** in its rightful place. *That* place that God chose to create seed is in between dry land and the first forms of life. *God understood* that it takes seed with the capability to reproduce seed to form a never ending cycle of life.

Let me simplify *wha*t God meant when He said, "a fruit tree yielding fruit whose seed is in itself." That simply means if you pull an apple from a tree and cut it open, you should find seed in that apple. If you find seed in that apple and plant those seed, apple trees should begin to grow. Those new apple trees should grow up *and* bare apples-just like the apple that you cut open.

God proved the importance of seed by creating them

before He created anything else on earth. Now get ready, you are about to understand why Satan wants control of all seed that has the ability to sustain human life. It is simple, Satan knows how important it was to God and he wants control of all of it to destroy human life. Satan's plan is to sit back and watch patented seed dominate and destroy God's creation of seed. I believe Satan is very supportive of Monsanto's seed patents, especially the patented terminator gene. In this book there is a chapter written on the terminator gene. The terminator gene is a gene that causes a seed to destroy its own embryo. I have heard several different names given to the terminator gene, such as "plant gene expression", "seed sterility", and "altered fertility." All of these terms have the same meaning when the end results are reached.

My 21 year old seed business was closed as a result of Monsanto's monopoly tactics. I believe Satan is very proud of Monsanto's control and ability to destroy seed growers like me. If God gives me the ability to spoil Satan's laughter, it will be done with this book. I give you my word, Satan wishes that this seed takeover to be secretive and I believe his intentions is to keep this a secret. He simply plans to have the control of the seed patents made ready for him to easily acquire during the great tribulation.

Now that you understand that seed controls food in all human life, let us go to the next level of understanding. That understanding will come from the giant seed company, Monsanto, and their unbelievable requirements for farmers who purchase and use their seed. I believe that Monsanto's patenting technology has over 90 percent of American farmers caught up in its web. These farmers are not evil people. It is almost impossible for farmers to survive in America without joining Monsanto's technology "stewardship program."

If you understand what I have written so far, you are on your way to understanding that the **666's** are in the seed. With the understanding and knowledge given to me by God, I'll now thrust my hand into the heart of Monsanto's secrets, rip it out, and lay them across the pages of this chapter and book.

I'll hit hard from the beginning and tell you that the anti-Christ will use seed to control nations and its people. He will also use seed to create food shortages which will make his mark (666) or his number a very desirable item.

The scary part of the deceptions of this monster seed plan is that it is not detected by many people, including Christians, farmers, lawyers, Bible scholars, clergy and devout prophecy preachers. During the last few years, I have constantly watched religious shows on television and have not heard one speaker mention this seed control scenario. I did, however, watch a documentary on LINK television about a tribe of Indians in Minnesota. Some of these Indians were interviewed about being told they couldn't harvest wild rice anymore because some company had patented them. I could see the pain on these native Americans' faces as they told of their ancestors harvesting wild rice for thousands of years. One tribal leader referred to the patenting of wild rice being immoral because the Creator had placed it on earth for people to use. This was the first statement I have heard connecting God, the Creator, to patented seed. One native American lady actually mentioned the terminator gene on this documentary. I perceived her to have greater knowledge than she was allowed to express in her allotted time on camera.

It is a secret wrapped in other secrets with many of the world's most important people giving it a stamp of approval. God will unwrap those secrets and help me to expose the importance of this seed plan in this book. I'll simply provide a 190 pound, 50 plus year-old vessel for Him to use. I fully understand that I can be killed for this.

A Monsanto Technology seed salesman issued me a

carefully worded death threat in 2003 when I caught up with him putting one of their signs in my field illegally. I made him take the sign down and stand in front of a video camera and apologize for putting the sign up. When I first noticed the sign one morning, I felt sure it had just been put up that day. I called the salesman assigned to our area and he told me on the cell phone that he had not put a sign up in my area in two weeks. I asked him to come to the field immediately and he agreed to do so. In approximately 30 minutes he drove up to the field, climbed out of his truck, and told me he had put the sign up a couple of days before and had forgotten about it. I felt like he was lying because I was 100 percent sure the sign wasn't even up earlier that morning. I had not had much luck aiming cameras in Monsanto's private investigators' faces because they just get mad and get in their trucks and leave without saying much. Because of that I decided to be very nice to this Monsanto salesman and see if I could talk him into admitting putting the sign on my field on camera. I knew syrup catches more flies than vinegar. The syrup worked and he took down the sign and admitted to putting it up. He told me that a farmer who farmed adjacent fields had told him that the field was his. I guess this salesman didn't know that the adjacent fields were farmed by me also. The farmer who the salesman claimed to be talking about told me later the salesman came to him and tried to get him to go along with his story. The farmer said he refused to do so. I believe this was a scheme of entrapment where Monsanto could snap pictures of their sign on my field and two or three years down the road use it in court and say, "Michael White was advertising our seed and here's pictures of a sign on his field to prove it." If that was their plan, the plan fell through when the fly lit on the syrup.

I set the camera on top of my Jeep, pointed in another direction and the salesman began to talk in a manner I would call scary, yet also threatening and deceptive. He informed me that one man in Tupelo, Mississippi, had already been killed in a mysterious manner. He said the man was found dead after a group of men drove up and went into a building where the man was. He said the man was apparently choked to death, but the investigation was swept under the rug. He stated that he just wanted me to be aware of what I was dealing with. He said this man worked with Mitchell Scruggs of Tupelo, Mississippi, who was also sued by Monsanto. This weighed heavy on my mind and a few mornings later I left at approximately 3:30 in the morning in a different vehicle and drove to Tupelo, Mississippi, and talked to Mitchell Scruggs about the situation. Mr. Scruggs told me this man knew better than to tell a story like that. He said his worker apparently died when a bail of cotton fell on him. This was the first time I had met Mr. Scruggs so I did not know him very well. I still had severe reservations about whether or not Mr. Scruggs was scared and didn't know me well enough to share a very lengthy conversation with me. I personally knew what it felt like not to trust anyone if you didn't completely know their background. Mr. Scruggs could have very easily had reservations about whether or not I was telling him the truth. After the years have passed and my lawyers and Mr. Scruggs' lawyers have worked together I had grown to know and admire Mitchell Scruggs. He is a warrior in the battle against Monsanto. He has spent several million dollars in litigation costs taking on this billion dollar giant. The Monsanto seed salesman's warning did not really surprise me because of certain scriptures.

Jesus also has warned me in Matthew 24:9 {KJV}] Then shall they deliver you up to be afflicted, and shall kill you: and ye shall be hated of all nations for my name's sake.

I fully understand that Monsanto could kill me if they so desire to and God allows them to. After this book hits the market for the world to read, Monsanto's hate for me will multiply. They will, however, have to deal with a man that fears Almighty GOD ... not man.

As you begin to understand this book, we'll elaborate on Monsanto's policies, which they call "good stewardship." They want all farmers to be a so-called good steward. The truth is that their verison of a good steward forces the farmers to comply with their rules, and places billions of dollars into their own pockets.

I do not level any harsh words at any farmer who has knowingly or unknowingly signed a Monsanto stewardship agreement. I do not level any condemnation on the vast majority of the people who work for Monsanto, or other seed companies that produce patented seed. I do, however, put my finger in the face of lawyers and corporate executives who know and promote the deception of this seed plan.

I want to make this statement very clear, "I do not call anyone associated with Monsanto, or any other large seed company the anti-Christ." I do not have any idea who the anti-Christ is, or what nation, or profession he will come from. I will make this statement, however, "patented seed will become the most prized possession of the anti-Christ". The anti-Christ will take over existing laws and use these laws that are beneficial to him. When the anti-Christ takes over world laws he will instantly own these patented seed laws.

Please try to understand as I prioritize this seed takeover and its power and effectiveness. Humans have to have food, food comes from seed, seed now comes largely from patented seed and patented seed has become law. Now, do you see, knowing his ability to take over laws, how he will acquire control of seed?

We are now going to pierce the veil of Monsanto's deception and intentions. My source that I will use to unmask Monsanto with is the GIFT of the scrapbook that they mailed to me in 2004. This is a very complex, well-oiled machine of deception.

The first sheet of paper I'll use to open the first wound carries their name with the logo at the top of the paper with the words, "FOOD, HEALTH, AND HOPE." Taking the first word, FOOD, diverts your attention from seed. They recently became a 100 percent seed technology orientated company.

The next word, HEALTH, fails to mention the possible health dangers of genetically modified food. The next word, HOPE, is anyone's guess as to the meaning of it. I believe that they hope to put the world on its knees, begging them for seed at any price.

The page that I am writing from has a number at the bottom "x17720622"--I do not know the meaning of this number. The only person's name on this paper is Scott B. Baucum. Under his name are three words, "Manager, **Value Capture.**"

The word **VALUE** means "the regard that something is held to deserve; importance or worth, material or monetary worth." The word **CAPTURE** means "taking or being taken by force, surprise, or skill." Monsanto loves to call a farmer who saves seed a **"pirate."** Mr. Baucum, it seems to me the word "pirate" applies to your job title much more than it applies to a farmer, after we put the dictionary meaning to your job title.

Mr. Baucum, when you met with Alabama State officials in 2003, some of those officials told me what you said about me. They said you told them there was a money deal for 74 out of 75 farmers, but not for me, Michael White. I was told that you wanted to make an example out of me, "a poster boy." I did not know what that meant and it scared me. I put my wife to bed that night crying at 10:30 p.m. That was the second time I had ever seen my wife cry in 21 years of marriage. Soon after that night my family, health, business, and sanity was almost totally destroyed. I hold your "poster boy" selection process responsible for all of that, including the frivolous suing of my elderly father. I watched him change my mother's diaper and cry at the same time over you suing him. You had thousands of farmers that you could have sued that have saved thousands of bushels of soybean seed. My father has never saved or planted a soybean seed in his life. In fact, he stopped farming many years before Monsanto ever got into the business of genetically altered seed.

You consider yourself an untouchable Goliath; let me tell you what you are with the meaning of your own words, "VALUE CAPTURE." You have proclaimed yourself as the person who has the right to take over God's creation of "seed " by any method possible: force, surprise, deception, including the destruction of men such as my Father. I pray I get to see you stand beside my father on judgement day, Baucum. I'll also issue this challenge, Baucum, I'll debate you live, unedited and uncensored on national television.

I'll now go to another letter in the GIFT package that I received from Monsanto. This letter carries the signature of Brian E. Coombs. Under his name is what I would call his job title. Those words are "intellectual property stewardship." Mr. Coombs makes several references to patent number 435. Mr. Coombs makes several references to saving and planting Monsanto's patented seed as being illegal; however, he failed to inform me that Monsanto would have investigators (seed police) coming to my business offering money to get me to do what he says not to do. It seems Monsanto has a double standard which entraps farmers and seed men.

He asked me to consult with council or state requirements concerning certain issues. In addition, he asked me to keep one half to one cup of farmers' seed in a sealed envelope. I would like to inform Mr. Coombs that I called in the state of Alabama USDA Inspector. They informed me that I was not required by law to obtain or keep a sample of any farmer's seed that came to my place of business.

Mr. Coombs, Monsanto sued me on patent number 605,

and you refer to 605 and 435. Why did you not sue me for 435? It is now a fact that 435 is worthless and you know it. Could patent 605 also be in danger of being ruled worthless?

Never in the history of society have farmers been accused of being pirates. Pirates have a definition of someone who robs or hijacks ships or other cargo or goods. These farmers are taken to courts which, most of the time, is in Monsanto's home town of St. Louis, MO. Farmers, when purchasing your seed, give up their right to a jury trial. They are forced before your so-called arbitration board. I do not know of any farmer who has won in your arbitration.

Since 1996, your company began selling your seed even if a farmer refused to sign a stewardship agreement. Your licenced salesmen sold many bags of your seed knowing full well they weren't requiring farmers to sign your technology agreements. One of your salesmen attempted to give me some of your patented seed, but I wouldn't take the bait. This incident happened after I was already sued by Monsanto. I know that Monsanto would now love to give me free seed and deceive me into planting them. Then they would run screaming to a Judge, "Look what Michael White has done!" Forget it, Baucum, it is not going to happen. A high percentage of farmers have always saved their own seed, which is a God-given right. I had one high-ranking university official in the year of 2003 tell me he did not know of any university in the U.S. ever suing a single farmer for one dollar.

These universities have thousands of varieties of "protected variety" seed on the market. One of your company's policies is to take money from settlements from farmers and give to the American Farm Bureau. On one of the letters that you mailed to me you have a logo "Monsanto and American Farm Bureau." You say that you give the Farm Bureau money for scholarships to give for students to pursue agriculture-related majors in accredited schools.

That is a very good plan to keep the American Farm Bureau off of your back, when you take money from farmers. You are more than welcome to use the pictures of my elderly Father and Mother to show these farm families, and the American Farm Bureau. I am not going to copyright the pictures of my Father and my Mother. She died during the lawsuit, but you are still welcome to use them to show how willing you are to sue anyone.

I have a 21 year old daughter in college, and if you gave me a million dollar check of your captured money, I would love to burn it and let the smoke go up your nostrils. You listed a man by the name of Brett Begemann as the Vice President of Monsanto. His sugar coated words are "we are proud to contribute funds received from seed settlements and invest them in the future of these young men and women." Mr. Begemann is welcome to carry the pictures of my Father and Mother to colleges and show these students where some of this money comes from. They haven't taken any money from my father and I don't believe they will be able to.

I have never dealt with men as heartless as some of Monsanto's officials, lawyers, and investigators. American Farm Bureau should be ashamed to take money from a company like Monsanto. You are also welcome to make posters of my Mother and Father and place them in your offices. I honestly do not care if you enlarge these pictures to cover a whole wall and put them in every office that you have. You take the money and you don't have the guts to show where it comes from. I just called your bluff and you put your head into the sand.

On one of these pages Monsanto boasts of a jury verdict in Louisiana, costing a cotton grower 1.6 million dollars and giving it to Monsanto. It also says that the jury gave 400 thousand dollars of this grower's money to another company. They say that the jury awarded reasonable royalties. In the same paragraph they say that this jury's decision sent shock waves through the South. My question is why does something reasonable send shock waves?

Farmers have to have a six digit I.D. card to purchase and use Monsanto's seed. Farmers have no choice with 87 percent of the 2005 soybean crop being under Monsanto's laws. I call this card an agriculture mark of the beast card. When I make this statement, I do not mean that it has any religious bearing on a person's standing with God. It is just that Monsanto has developed a six (6) digit system to buy and sell their seed, or seed products with. Do not blame me Monsanto, but I cannot help but to notice that 6's keep falling upon your head.

You, the reader, look at web sites or use your phone to gain knowledge of seed stewardship. One of the papers that Monsanto sent to me says that they want you to keep informed. I'll list the three phone numbers that they gave to me. For fax or e-mail, call 1-888-235-4332, ext. 3382. Anyone with questions on stewardship should call 1-800-768-6387 or 314-694-1261.

I hope that this first chapter has enlightened you as to what is going on in the seed world, which directly effects your world. We will leave this chapter now and go into a book which I do not feel worthy to write and I give full credit to God. These are the last days of the last days. So do yourself a favor by reading and understanding that "the 666's are in the seed".... All that I, Michael White, ask of you is to prove me wrong.

2 The Terminator Gene

God put seed on the earth before He put anything else. The reason for that is very easy to understand when you put common sense to work. Seed is the locomotive that pushes and pulls the food train. The creator and owner of this seed train has always been God. God gave it to humans so that it would constantly replenish without any interference by man. By the time you read the first twelve verses of Genesis, the word "seed" is mentioned four times.

*Genesis 1:11 (KJV) And God said, Let the earth bring forth grass, the herb yielding **seed**, [and] the fruit tree yielding fruit after his kind, whose **seed** [is] in itself, upon the earth: and it was so. {grass: Heb. tender grass}*

*12 And the earth brought forth grass, [and] herb yielding **seed** after his kind, and the tree yielding fruit, whose **seed** [was] in itself, after his kind: and God saw that [it was] good*

Let me reemphasize that God saw seed first and foremost to sustain all forms of life. Big corporations are claiming and patenting what God gave the human race. Without a doubt, these patents will be taken over by the anti-Christ when he comes to power in this world. Monsanto and other large companies are able to prosecute anyone who saves patented seed. However, they will not be able to keep these patents from coming under the command of the New World Leader.

In the late 1990's, a seed company named Delta and Pine Land Company received a patent on a gene commonly called the "Terminator Gene." I believe the patent number is 5,723,765.

Sometime during the late 1990's, Monsanto attempted to purchase Delta and Pine Land Company. I believe if Monsanto succeeds in the acquisition of Delta and Pine Land Company, they will gain at least 50 percent control of the terminator gene patent which is also called "plant gene expression."

In recent years Monsanto has exerted great efforts and finances in an attempt to purchase Delta and Pine Land Company. The use of this patent gives its owner the right to engineer a seed which will have a sterile embryo. Throughout history, Satan has always tried to kill the male seed (example: Jesus and Moses). Use of a seed system that prevents second generation germination makes it impossible for anyone to save seed that will emerge from the ground.

Remember, even Jesus had to emerge from the grave to complete the harvest; His germination took 72 hours. Seventy-two hours is the ideal time frame for a seed to germinate and emerge from the ground.

The common name of the seed fathered by patent number 5,723,765 "Terminator Gene" automatically makes you think of a woman terminating her pregnancy, which is the killing or destruction of the embryo.

Causing a seed to have a sterile embryo is in direct contrast to seed having seed in itself (Genesis 1:11). An embryo-killing gene such as this is created by man, not God. I would hate to place myself in a position for monetary gain that would cause me to have a part in the introduction of the Terminator Gene.

None of my words in this book are worthy to be written in red. The woes in the 23rd chapter of Matthew step forward in the face of the men who promote the Terminator Gene. Many men have a much deeper knowledge of the Terminator Gene than I do. I'll let these men speak from the laboratory and I'll speak from the spiritual and biblical danger of such a gene.

Making seeds hybrid has been in existence for years. Hybridizing seed has mostly been used in corn seed. Terminator seed and hybrid seed serve the same purpose, but differ in the method each one uses. Termination kills a seed's embryo and hybridization will allow a seed to have an embryo and sprout and come out of the ground. The problem a farmer encounters if he plants a saved hybrid seed is that it yields very little, if any. Several major crops such as wheat, rice, soybeans and cotton that I've had experiences with are not hybridized.

In the photo section of this book there's a picture (#2) of a genetically modified stalk of corn that volunteered in a soybean field in 2004 (Volunteering is when a seed accidently survives the winter and sprouts and comes up the following growing season). This stalk grew from a genetically modified hybridized seed. This stalk of corn had ample nutrients, moisture and conditions to yield its full potential. Nevertheless its full potential yielded only two damaged kernels of corn. A normal ear of corn should yield approximately 600 healthy kernels of corn; I personally do not see the need for the terminator gene to be used in corn. Corn has already been hybridized to the point that if anyone saved seed from it, the yield would be near zero.

I'm not aware of Monsanto suing anyone for the saving of corn seed. They only sue people who save seed that have reproductive capabilities. Monsanto has a near-perfect win record in the court system. However, many experts believe the ice is getting thinner under their feet. As I sit here today writing this chapter, I feel blessed to have been given the green light to a jury trial; I am told by experts that I am the first farmer out of

600 to make it this far. Monsanto claims to want this before a jury, but they use unbelievable tactics to prevent it from going to a jury trial. Monsanto knows that all giants fall and so they have to be afraid of this case. I also believe Monsanto has fear of Mitchell Scruggs' case in Mississippi because Mr. Scruggs can stand toe to toe with them financially. He has a team of expert patent lawyers whose knowledge is helping me in my case.

Introduction of the terminator gene has a multi-purpose capability. One of these capabilities is certain to cause farmers to have to purchase new seed every year. A seed with a terminated or sterile embryo would be worthless for planting. This would result in an enormous price increase for seed. You can certainly see the profit potential for Monsanto to introduce the terminator gene.

For all farmers and vegetable growers to have to purchase new seed, such as wheat, rice, and soybeans, will result in staggering profits in major seed companies. I believe other large seed companies are involved in the introduction of the terminator gene. I was in the seed business for 21 years, until Monsanto forced me out in 2004.

Almost any farmer who came to my place of business in 2003 was stalked, harassed, or received threatening letters from Monsanto. The last three large farmers who brought 18-wheeler loads of seed to me to be cleaned all received a threatening letter from Monsanto. These farmers had non-genetically modified seed. Monsanto knew the result of mailing these letters. The result was that these farmers were scared away from my place of business. These were men that I did business with for years. They were bringing me conventional seed and it was none of Monsanto's business. Monsanto mails out these types of letters as a fear tactic; none of these three men were sued by Monsanto. Nevertheless theses letters served their purpose, to put me out of business. Methods such as this raised a red flag and helped cause this book to be written. Swallow the bitter pill, Monsanto, your own actions helped write this book. Thanks!

You, the readers, understand the facts; Monsanto's seed patents, destroying of the competition, and the terminator gene are a dangerous recipe humanity has not faced before. With permission from GOD, I will make the statement that actions such as the above will be very instrumental in causing Matthew 24:21 to be fulfilled: *"For then shall be great tribulation, such as was not since the beginning of the world to this time, no, nor ever shall be."*

It is easy for us to understand that GOD created the earth, light, dry land, then seed in the beginning. For us to understand that these events have already happened, we must now understand that these events, according to the Scripture, will be partially or totally destroyed in the near future.

As I searched the scriptures that would apply to what I have experienced with the lawsuits, surveillance of my family and myself, my customers, and my seed company, I began to receive some answers. I had to first look at the facts. The facts are God's seed is being altered and farmers are being sued for saving seed, which is unprecedented in the history of the world. Surveillance on farmers and seedmen compare to what post-rapture destruction of the Bible will be. Considering these facts that I was fortunate enough to experience, I questioned, "What next?"

The terminator gene would not leave my mind for some reason. Even though my lawsuit did not pertain to the terminator gene, I could not understand why my mind was dwelling on it. I began to search the scriptures for any evidence of the terminator gene lying hidden in the scripture. I was experiencing post-rapture conditions, including fearing for my life. I had already suffered destroyed health, family, business and a nervous breakdown. Why was all of this happening and why was I being led to write a book with a title such as the title of this book?

I simply had to look up to God and tell Him to show me the terminator gene in the scriptures. I started in the book of Revelation and ended up in Genesis. I uncovered many interesting facts that are important to human existence. People do not have to have God to live, but they do have to have seed. If you just told yourself I shouldn't place seed over God, let me explain. People live their lives without God and go to hell at the rate of one person per second. None of these people lived their lives without being sustained by the final product of seed, which is food. That fact is how I can put seed over God by His permission and backed up by the fact that seed was His first gift to humanity. Without a doubt, if God saw the importance of seed to be His first gift to humans, the anti-Christ will certainly wish to take seed away first. My prayers go out for the people who, unaware, helped push this dangerous seed system forward. For those in the system who know what they are a part of, let God deal with you. This book is written for Christians and non-Christians alike. It is written as a wake-up call to the fact that the end is prepared for its marriage supper to the anti-Christ. Seed will be the main finger food at the marriage supper of the anti-Christ and the false prophet.

I know it seems foolish to many who read this book from a professional standpoint that patented seed, including the terminator gene, will be connected to a person called the anti-Christ. Many people from the biogenetic world do not believe in him anyway. He is simply a fictional character they may or may not have heard of. There are many people reading this book just because you've heard it may have an effect on your corporation or personal finances. It is unknown to me the effect it will have on society. We have become a very technologically enlightened society that wishes to genetically modify (clone) even human seed.

You, the professional scoffers who laugh at the very possibility and existence of the anti-Christ and the battle of Armageddon, are unknowingly volunteering to join him and fight against Jesus. I don't intend for this book's main focus to be the anti-Christ. The main focus is patented seed. Many people have already written books about the anti-Christ and I won't attempt to match wits with the authors. I feel I have been given a task to expose the hijacking of the worldwide seed supply. Genetically modified crops grew 25-fold from 1996 to the year 2000. The patenting and altering of seed have the capability to provide control or destruction of the food chain.

You, the brilliant inventors, and owners of the terminator gene–in search of the scriptures, I found your gene hidden in a totally agricultural verse. Your present attempt to change the name of the terminator gene to seed sterility helps confirm the Scripture. This is probably the most important Scripture that GOD has given me to authenticate this book; the scripture is Joel 1:17.

Joel 1:17 (KJV) The seed is rotten under their clods, the garners are laid desolate, the barns are broken down; for the corn is withered.

I would like to write this book, and especially this chapter, with my face buried on the floor. I am not worthy to write about such a matter as deep and factual as this. I did not volunteer for this, yet I did. I know that sentence did not make any sense to the average reader, but I had to pen it anyway.

The time has come for me to explain Joel 1:17. Joel's writing and speaking took place 2800 years ago. Joel is speaking of a terrible time and agony upon man and beast. You the sinner, you the Christian, you the genetic manipulators, journey with me through this scripture and prove me wrong if you can.

Joel was speaking of a plague which is a prophetic symbol of the day of the Lord (tribulation), which is the terror of God's approaching judgment day. This verse is totally agricultural and it is totally tribulation-era period. He said the seed is rotten under their clods. For a seed or anything else to rot under the surface of the ground it has to have moisture.

Joel said that the garners lay desolate. A garner in Joel's day was a hand sickle. A hand sickle was a three-foot blade attached to a handle and used to cut or garner the grain. That was the garner that he was speaking of. A garner in today's time frame would be a grain harvesting machine commonly called a combine. I have provided for you in the photo section a picture (#5) of myself holding a sickle along with one of my combines. Joel is saying that everything you see in this picture will not operate during the tribulation.

"The barns are broken down," was his prophetic vision of modern-day grain elevators going out of use. Joel's barns were store houses for grain. In our time frame it would be grain storage facilities. I have provided for you in the photo section a picture{#4}of the largest grain facility in the county in which I live being torn down in 2004. I live in Jackson County in northeast Alabama, other grain storage facilities are in the process of being torn down also.

"The corn is withered" in the field was his vision of what saved corn seed does today. I have already explained what a modern day saved corn seed will do. Refer to the photo section picture (#2).

If you noticed a contrast in him saying "the seed is rotten under their clods," yet the corn germinated and came up out of the ground, there is a reason. The corn seed had to sprout and come up to wither. If you save seed from modern-day genetically modified or hybrid seed corn, it does exactly what Joel said it would do-it withers in the field. Corn has no need for the "terminator gene" and I have also gained knowledge that for some unknown reason corn will not except the "terminator gene".

Seed patents under the control of the anti-Christ and seed with the terminator gene will, without a doubt, fulfill Joel's prophesy. These two happenings will automatically cause the combines (garners) and the barns (grain elevators) to go unused.

Let us return to the fourth word of the verse which is "rotten." A seed has to receive moisture before it can rot. If a seed receives moisture and has a good embryo, it will not rot. A good embryo means good germination. Good germination causes a seed to emerge from the ground and grow. If a seed did not receive any moisture, it would lie under the soil and exist with its embryo intact until moister came. We have now established the fact that if Joel's seed, which seems to mean all seed, is rotten under the clods, there has to be something wrong with them. We have now decided that the seed that Joel saw has a terrible germination problem. That problem has to lie in the embryo. This means that the embryo of the seed that Joel saw has to be sterile. Succinctly causing a seed to be sterile is the terminator gene's sole purpose.

Having a "lab test" preformed on seed is a method in which a laboratory determines what percent germination a sample of seed has. Almost all samples of seed I have had tested in laboratories average a germination rate of almost 90 percent. This means that if Joel's seed were normal and in the ground and had sufficient moisture, nine out of ten of his seed should come up. I dedicate this next statement to the brilliant inventors of the terminator gene. The seed Joel prophetically saw had a sterile embryo. You, the inventor of the terminator gene, Joel saw your seed 2800 years before you did.

Ownership of the terminator gene, and possessing a conscience that would permit you to use this gene, automatically places you against God. If God would have wanted seed embryos destroyed then *Genesis 1:12* would not have been written in the Bible. To the owners of the terminator gene, you have just been placed in battle with God and His Word. One of you will be found wrong. Tell me you brilliant beings of flesh, who like myself are on your way to the grave, "who is right, you or God?"

From the writings of the so-called experts, I find confusion and inconsistencies. The truth is, they don't know what effects the terminator gene will have on nature. It seems no one knows the end result and they are simply willing to take a chance on it by releasing it, thus risking our entire food supply.

I have given them the benefit of the doubt, yet their uncertainty has caused me to take Joel's prophecy for fact. When reading *Joel 1:17,* I did not find the word "if" in his statements. He spoke with authority and a revelation from God. You, the experts, who want to guess at the terminator gene's effects on the world's eco system, sit down-you're not worthy to play around with God's creation. Let me rephrase that last sentence and tell you to keep standing up so the scriptures can be fulfilled.

In the past two or three years, I have been reading warning labels pertaining to the purchase and use of seed that warns you about pollen flow. Farmers are signing papers that they will control pollen flow. If I stood two genetic scientists in a field with their noses one inch apart, they could not control the flow of pollen between their noses. I believe that these warnings about pollen flow are a safety-net for the inventors of dangerous genetically modified pollen. Those overlooked warnings will help turn the blame on the farmer in a "we warned you" or "we told you so" manner. I have read from some large seed companies' warnings that in most cases pollen only travels a few feet. Using binoculars, I have sat in the mountains of Northwest Colorado many mornings as the sun came up and watched pollen blow horizontally from one mountain to another. Some of these mountains are several miles apart.

Wind direction, and the velocity of wind, greatly determines the distance pollen flows. Moisture conditions, such as rainy or dry weather, have a great impact on pollen movement. We all know many insects, especially bees of many different types, are involved in the movement of pollen. Insects such as bees are part of God's plan to pollinate seed-bearing plants and trees miles apart. I guess you, the men who plan to introduce the terminator gene, will tell the bees and other insects they are not allowed to carry this pollen.

Introduction of all of these genetically altered genes is fueled by greed and money. When you look at the pictures of my father and mother in this book, you will understand the degrees of greed Monsanto lives by. Then begin to understand Monsanto has no heart in enforcing these patents on the human race. My father has never sat on a tractor and planted a soybean in his life. Even if he had saved a few soybeans for seed, what type of person or corporation would put an elderly man through agony the remaining years of his life?

If need be, I'll roll my elderly father into the courtroom in a hospital bed. As bad as I hate to admit it, I still have to give you thanks for suing him. Him being the oldest man in the history of the world to be sued for saving seed has been very instrumental in helping me write this book. You, the heartless men who made the decision to sue him, put the gunstock against your shoulder next time... instead of the barrel.

As I sat in Federal deposition in 2004, a feeling came over me that I was unaccustomed to. I entered that deposition holding on to the scripture that the Spirit would give me the words to say in that hour. Luke 12:11-12 (KJV)

Luke 12:11 And when they bring you unto the synagogues, and [unto] magistrates, and powers, take ye no thought how or what thing ye shall answer, or what ye shall say: 12 For the Holy Ghost shall teach you ***what ye ought to in the same hour say.***

I silently questioned God about the feelings that came over me concerning these lawyers, then I realized I was sitting before men that chose to take upon themselves to take over the world's seed supply.

I temporally visualized the countless millions of men, women, and children that would go hungry or receive the mark during tribulation because of these men's present-day actions. Then I began to understand the feeling that was upon me was of God. I was not allowed to show these men any mercy or fear. They chose their own arena and future. Their place in eternity will be a result of their own actions. If they repent and become Christians, so be it. If they spend their eternity in hell, so be it. I was told by the Spirit if I witnessed to them I would be laughed at and silenced by them. I then realized that it was ordained for us to be enemies for this time period. I truly believe it would be a sin for me to bow down to them. During the deposition, certain circumstances sealed the title of this book to its cover. This title had given me problems, but their words and actions erased any doubt as to what I should title this book. We never discussed the terminator gene and I am sure they had no knowledge of this book being written. Their methods of silencing farmers would be used to the extreme on me if they had knowledge of this book.

To write this book I have looked at the spiritual ground in front of me, and place my foot in a footprint already made for me by God. My knowledge on the genetic make-up of the terminator gene is limited to the fact that it simply causes a seed to destroy its own embryo, therefore rotting in the ground and never bearing seed, like Joel said.

I do know that the pollen from the terminator gene is not limited to its own species; in other words, I believe it is possible for terminator gene crops to produce pollen that can be transferred by wind, insects, ground, and possibly many other methods of travel for countless miles.

We, the farmers of North Alabama in 2005, are having to spray our soybean fields to prevent Asian soybean rust from killing our fields. We are being told that this rust came in from overseas, riding on the 2004 hurricanes. If that be the case, tell me what will prevent the terminator gene pollen from traveling worldwide, and tell me why the anti-Christ will not acquire this as his genetic atomic weapon to destroy food, which the Black horse in Revelation 6:6 guarantees to happen. Prove me wrong, you the owner and the introducer of the terminator gene. I feel safe because you will have to go through God's Word and the Prophet Joel and the book of Revelation to do so. I rest my case, so start your attack, non believers.

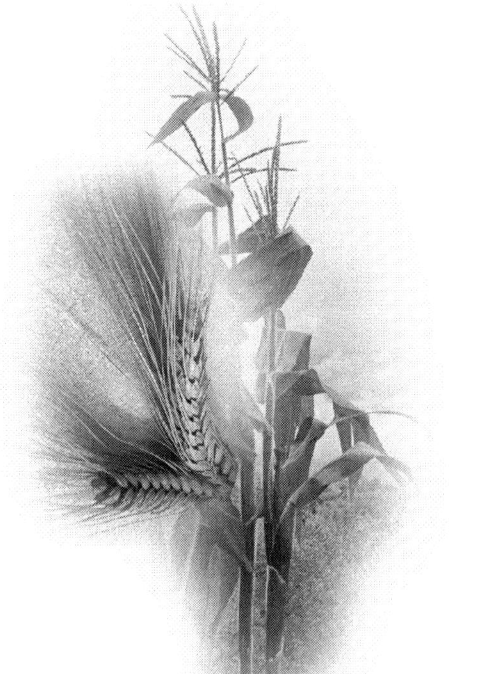

3 The Dream

During the year 2002, I had a dream. I do not remember the exact month. This dream was one of the most scary, and most realistic dreams I have ever had. The dream took place before I ever spoke before a congregation. I would consider it more than just a dream, perhaps a half-dream, half-vision.

It took place around 2:30 in the early hours of the morning. In the dream I was carried out into a green, grassy field by someone and sat down on an old wooden chair. I did not get to see who carried and directed me. I cannot say if it was a person, spirit, or just a voice directing me.

I was seated in the chair and told that the Great White Throne Judgment was beginning to take place, just over toward my right side. I was given strict orders not to look in that direction. I had the freedom to turn and look, but knew I shouldn't because of the serious tone in the entity's voice. I believe I felt the same way Lot's wife felt in Genesis 19:17 when God warned her not to look back at the city of Sodom.

Gen 19:17 {KJV} And it came to pass, when they had brought them forth abroad, that he said, Escape for thy life; look not behind thee, neither stay thou in all the plain; escape to the mountain, lest thou be consumed.

I could hear voices coming from my right-hand side, but I could not distinguish the exact words. To my left, not more than a mile's distance from me, was a great burning expanse I knew to be Hell. The opening was wide and looked to be more than thirty miles in diameter at the top. It appeared to be like a volcano in reverse. It reminded me of how water runs out of a bathtub. The little vortex created as the water runs down the drain. However, this wasn't mere water, this was a thirty mile-wide downward spiral of liquid fire similar to a volcano's red hot lava. As it churned, I could see hundreds of thousands, if not millions, of people rolling in and out of the hot mass of fire and being sucked into its vortex. Their screams could be heard individually, yet there were so many of them that it also echoed and blended into a giant roar of terrible pleas for help.

Fear and panic seized my heart and I became nauseous, sickened by the thought that these people were just beginning eternity. Also, I began to wonder if I had actually died and this chair was just my temporary resting place before I would be called to the judgment throne.

I looked up to see three men walking in front of me. The one in the center was in deep agony. He was being escorted by two other men, one on each side. I realized that he had just been judged and was being escorted toward Hell for eternity. Then others came by, just as before, with two huge men escorting someone in the middle. These men, or whatever they were, doing the escorting reminded me of a very elite team of very physically fit athletes or maybe they were huge prison guards. They were all the same size, about 6' 8", and weighing about 280 or 300 pounds, very muscular and stocky. Even their facial features looked similar. They were dressed in black, similar to a swat team or some riot team outfits. They carried no guns or weapons, but I quickly discovered they did not need any. This was the plan and will of God, so there was no one who could overpower these huge men or even cause them to step out of ranks.

As I sat there, hundreds of these teams passed about 20 feet in front of me. For some unknown reason, I did not know or could not figure out if these men worked for God or Satan. I even let my mind drift ahead and wondered where these men would go after the Great White Throne of Judgment was finalized. Were they angels, God's soldiers, or Satan's enforcement army to make certain that all recipients of the diploma of Hell made it there? To this day I have not figured out which side these men were on.

Thousands of these teams passed, like an army of ants, marching men and women to their eternal doom. Each step was like military precision, marching toward the mouth of the giant spiral of fire. As they neared the entrance, I could tell that the heat was very intense, because the person in the middle started screaming way before they arrived. Then, as they reached Hell's doorway, they lifted the person and cast them into the flames. The people struggled, but they were no-match for the strength and size of these men. I could now see why these men were so big and strong.

Then, without breaking a stride, they turned and went back for someone else. There were two lines, as far as I could see, one carrying a person there, and another line of the men returning back to get another poor doomed soul. How many could it hold? Now I understand the scripture in Isaiah 5:14-16.

Isaiah 5 [KJV]:*14 Therefore hell hath enlarged herself, and opened her mouth without measure: and their glory, and their multitude, and their pomp, and he that rejoiceth, shall descend into it. 15 And the mean man shall be brought down, and the mighty man shall be humbled, and the eyes of the lofty shall be humbled: 16 But the LORD of hosts shall be exalted in judgment, and God that is holy shall be sanctified in righteousness.* As these teams passed by me I was able to see the sorrowful and lost expression on the faces of their captives, but none of them actually looked at me or acknowledged that I was there. I wondered why none of them seemed to see me. That's when I began to really believe that I was dead and my life back on earth was over. I wanted to scream out to someone back on earth, especially my wife. I wanted to ask her to tell me what was happening, but I remained silent because I knew no one would answer or hear me. I simply sat there as I was told to do.

Then all of a sudden, I heard one of the men that was being carried to Hell speak to one of the soldiers. He said, Look, let's stop and talk this over. I left a whole lot of money back on earth. Let me go back to earth and I'll get you any amount you want, and I promise I'll bring it back and give it to you. Just please don't keep dragging me toward Hell. Please, you can have all the money I have. Just a little more time on earth will give me a chance to get right with God while I'm back on earth getting you the money. The soldiers acted like they did not even know he was talking, they just kept on dragging him along.

Then I began to hear another person. He yelled at his captors, "Look, I'm a very important person back on earth. I'm a State Senator. You don't have the power to do this to me." But still the soldiers marched on toward Hell, again ignoring all of his shouts. They either did not hear him or did not care. I realized that these people being escorted from the Judgment Seat could see Hell just like I could.

The urge to look to my right was almost overwhelming, I wanted to know if anyone I knew was in line waiting to be judged. But I remembered Lot's wife and her judgment for looking back, turning her into a pillar of salt. There was no way I was going to look.

Then a third voice could be heard. He pleaded, "Hey, if either of you has ever watched TV, you've probably seen me. I've played in a lot of movies. Let's talk this over. I really think when you understand how famous I am, you'll let me go back to earth." Again, the soldiers ignored him and dragged him on by.

Another voice cried out as their team came by me.

He moaned, "I can't believe this is really happening. I always believed there was a God and a heaven and a hell. But I wasn't serious enough to do anything about it." Then he became silent, as if accepting his eternal fate. I watched for a while and he never said another word as they walked him toward Hell. I had to admire something in him, at least he accepted and admitted his mistakes and seemed to walk bravely toward the flames, knowing he would be there forever.

Coming up behind me a fifth man screamed and struggled against the soldiers to get free, but they simply lifted him off the ground by his arms and carried him. All the way I watched him fight and struggle until they threw him in. His soldiers seemed to be stronger than the others even though they looked just like the rest.

A sixth man passed by crying out something to his captors, but for some reason I did not hear or remember what he said. I only knew that he spoke to them and again they ignored him completely. Even though I don't know what he said, his words have bothered me for some time. I have always wondered what he said and why I was not permitted to hear or remember him. Who is it? Is it someone reading this book right now? The sixth man was sent to be a messenger to someone holding this book right now, a message straight from GOD to YOU. Please ask yourself what you would tell the soldiers if they were dragging you to hell! God's Spirit is upon me and I can feel the chills wash over my body. I know this is for someone reading these words. God's Spirit has also revealed to me that you know in your heart what you would say to these men. Let me emphasize one last point before I go on with this story. If you did say anything to the soldiers in your heart, then more than likely you are not ready to meet God. If so, please kneel right now and ask God to forgive you. I personally do not plan on ever being led away by these soldiers so I don't have anything to say to them.

I am ready to die and be judged. To die is gain and be with the Lord forever.

Phil 1:21{KJV} For to me to live is Christ, and die is gain.

Then another man came by me, the seventh man that I was permitted to hear speak. God tells me that this man is the reason many of you are reading this book. As the team of soldiers came by leading him, I heard him speak. Remember, I saw thousands being led by but was only permitted to hear seven speak. This seventh man walked more calmly than the others, more in step with the soldiers. I had not clearly seen the full face of anyone being carried to Hell. However, this man I was able to see completely. He only said a few words but I heard them distinctly. He said, "I knew this was going to happen to me if I didn't do what I was supposed to do." Then he turned and looked straight at me; he had MY face. The seventh man was ME!

Just as I realized his identity I woke up from the dream-vision. My sheets were drenched with sweat. I ran to the refrigerator and got a two-litter bottle of cola and drank as much as I could. I thanked God for letting me still be alive on earth, with the chance to do what I am supposed to do. This book is a big part of God's calling for my life.

In my dream-vision, I didn't get to the point where I lifted my eyes in Hell like the rich man did in Luke 16:22-24 (KJV):

22 "And it came to pass, that the beggar died, and was carried by the angels into Abraham's bosom: the rich man also died, and was buried; 23 And in Hell he lift up his eyes, being in torments, and seeth Abraham afar off, and Lazarus in his bosom. 24 And he cried and said, Father Abraham, have mercy on me, and send Lazarus, that he may dip the tip of his finger in water, and cool my tongue; for I am tormented in this flame.

I realize now that I was only given a glimpse of Hell so that I could tell others what I saw. They say a dream only lasts for a few seconds, but this one was longer. It seemed like it was several minutes long. I often work hard manual labor and seldom sweat. So I know I did not drench half the bed in just a few seconds.

I didn't immediately tell anyone else about the dream-vision, but after several months I told my wife and now I see even more reasons to reveal what I saw. I believe God will use this dream to win many souls. I know it was from God, a message straight from Him.

There is one last part of the dream that I chose to tell about at the end, although this occurred throughout the entire dream. I saw demons standing just at the edge of Hell awaiting the people being cast in. The demons ranged in size from over 10 feet tall to only a few inches. The largest demons were the most powerful. All were male, and all were nude. Every victim thrown in was immediately raped by several of these demons while they fought to stay above the torrents of the flames. It was so disgusting that it made me want to vomit. I saw several of the smaller demons trying to fight for the grasp of a new person, but they were not successful because the larger demons knocked them back every time. I believe the second largest demons were demons of power, money, and politics. The largest demons represented sexual immorality. I have no doubt now that sexual immorality will carry more people to Hell than anything else.

4 FEAR

As this chapter began to dance around the perimeter of my mind, I had difficulty in figuring out its title. My mind began to rethink some of the events that have happened over the past several years. My mind went back even to the early 90's when I heard a director at a state university speak at a seed meeting. This man said that the seed industry, as we had always known it, was going to change in the near future. At the time this meeting took place I had not heard of genetically modified seed. He assured us that the benefit to farmers would be an increased price for the genetically modified grain they produced.

It is somewhere close to ten years later now and during those ten years grain prices have fallen to levels from the 1950's and 1960's. These cheap prices are a result of overseas countries being afraid of the United States genetically altered food. As of 2005, the European Union has not granted approval for many of these commodities and grain. Farmers who buy many of these genetically modified seed have to agree to not sell the grain they produce to anyone who will ship the grain to countries that do not accept genetically modified food.

It seems that Monsanto, along with its fear tactics, also have successful, questionable tactics in many other areas. I personally have first-hand knowledge of their fear tactics. I still remember many memories of my family having fear of Monsanto's investigative tactics. This involved relentless stalking, picture taking, possible illegal phone taps, and a carefully worded death warning that I had received in 2003 from a licensed Monsanto seed salesman.

On the first Monday of September 2003, which was Labor Day, a very disturbing scenario began to develop. I was at Ider, Alabama, at the Ider Annual Mule Day. I was working a pair of mules and wagon in the parade at the start of the event. I had my wife and youngest daughter in the wagon with me. There were approximately 5,000 or more people lining the sides of the road for about a mile leading to where the event was taking place. These people were spectators who were watching the parade and would then come on to the city park where the activities were being held after the parade.

About mid-way through the parade, a man and a woman who looked to be in their forties to early fifties began calling my name, my wife's name, and my daughter's name. These two people's voice could be easily heard over the parade noise. I actually stopped a few feet from these people and they were laughing and calling out our names. They were wearing red, white and blue shirts and hats. My mind quickly turned to the thoughts of some of Monsanto's investigators having American flags on their trucks and SUV's. I believe Monsanto's investigators use patriotic symbols to lower suspicion about them. I asked my wife if she knew the man and woman and she said she didn't. I told her that I didn't know the people either and they might work for Monsanto. I saw the couple two more times during the day and they would wave at me and call out my name. At one point I actually parked my wagon and walked towards these people and they actually ran from me.

Four days after Labor Day, I was in Scottsboro, Alabama, on a Friday morning talking with a friend of mine about cutting timber. I was sitting in his truck when I noticed a new four-wheel drive truck circle the area a couple of times. On the second or third pass this truck made, I saw some type of camera being used in my direction by the passenger in this vehicle. I immediately instructed my friend to follow the truck, staying approximately one-fourth mile behind it. The truck pulled into a local lumber and hardware store. When we pulled into the parking lot, we immediately wrote down the tag number of the truck. The passenger had already gone into the store so I got out of the vehicle I was riding in and entered the store. I saw a lady standing at the checkout counter and assumed she was the one riding in the truck using a camera on me. I walked up behind her without her knowing I was there. She turned around as I walked up and it was without a doubt the lady who was at Ider Mule Day waving and calling out my name four days before.

I realized she probably recognized me so I turned and walked to the front of the store and entered the manager's office. It so happened that he was a good friend of mine and I asked him to monitor the lady and I would be back in a few minutes and talk to him. I told him I didn't have time to explain, but I would be back within a few minutes. I left the store, climbed into my friend's truck, and we drove down the street and waited until a truck carrying these two people left the hardware store parking lot. We drove back to the store and I went inside to talk to the manager. He said, Michael, that lady apparently knew you because she went to the window and watched you leave the parking lot. He said she then returned to the counter and wanted a key made, but did not want an invoice and wanted to pay cash for the key. He said he told her, sure, that he would make her a key for a dollar and wouldn't have to make an invoice on it. I quickly retrieved my office key from my pocket and asked the man who made the key if the blank key he used matched my office key and he said, "No." I then showed him my house key and he promptly said, "That's the key I made."

I ran from the store, jumped in the truck with my friend, and drove approximately one mile to the sheriff's office. As I was about the enter the sheriff's office, the sheriff drove up to me. I told him what had just happened and gave him the tag number of the truck. He began to put out the tag number over his radio to other officers. The tag number came back void, being registered to two separate vehicles approximately twelve years old in the state of Georgia. This was a new four-door diesel truck which I would estimate to be valued at $35,000 and it had a twelve year old tag that was suppose to be on a car. The sheriff put out a bolo (be on the lookout) on the vehicle to all city and county officers. The truck had already gotten out of the area and we haven't seen it since. Can I say Monsanto's investigators made a key to my house? No, I can't. I can, however, say this with 100 percent certainty: In the year 2003 the only people I caught taking pictures of me and running fake tags on new vehicles were those that worked for Monsanto. It is my belief that my office had already been entered into and if someone had a key to my house it may have very well been entered. I changed locks on my home several times because I had invoices on other farmers that I had placed in a safe location so that I could turn them in to Federal court if the judge ordered me to, which he did.

I am of the belief that if my invoices had come up stolen Monsanto would have run screaming to the judge that Michael White destroyed his invoices. I have knowledge that Monsanto uses private investigators that have worked different careers. I believe for that lady to be standing in that store with a key to my house a locksmith had to have made it for her. Four days prior when she and the man with her was watching me at Ider Mule Day it would have been a perfect time for someone to have been at my house making a key illegally. These people certainly knew my whereabouts most all the time, especially Labor Day 2003. I'll let you decide if you think this lady worked for Monsanto or not. Many events such as this caused a lot of fear to come upon me. Fear is a very dangerous handicap. I'm thankful that God has taken the element of fear from my mind and replaced it with some courage.

The tactics that Monsanto uses on farmers sends them into an immediate state of fear at the mention of their name. If I was only allowed one word to label Monsanto's personality other than evil, the word would be **"Draconian."** The word **Draconian** means **excessively harsh**, and its origin came from the Athenian legislator **Draco** (7th century B.C.). I can call this chapter a sister chapter to the one titled "Chants of the Giant." Monsanto has been very successful at using fear to force farmers to sign into Monsanto's agreements. They openly boast in their advertisements that they will sue you if you don't comply with all of their rules.

Throughout the Bible giants of evilness have lived by the sword and they have died by the sword. If Biblical history has taught me anything, Monsanto will die by the sword. I pray for God to find favor in me and provide me enough soldiers from many arenas to take their sword and thrust it through them, if it be His will. I made that statement with the first-hand knowledge that the element of fear is presently being turned upon Monsanto because of my trial being the first one out of several hundred to make it to a jury. I feel my fear of them going into remission or nonexistence. The reason for the feeling I now have is a result of a December 16, 2005, hearing in the Federal Courthouse in Huntsville, Alabama. On this day, my attorney received a call from the Federal Courthouse informing him he was suppose to be in Huntsville that very morning. My attorney's computer had apparently failed to receive an e-mail notifying him of this hearing. I believe the Federal Court e-mailed my attorney and some type of unintentional error prevented my lawyer from having knowledge of the hearing date and time.

We had just been appointed a new judge and did not know what to expect when we arrived in Huntsville. My attorney was very alarmed at being late for the hearing. That is a "no no" when it comes to any type of court hearing without notifying the court. To my lawyer's surprise, the judge was very lenient and waited close to an hour for my attorney to make the 45 mile trip. During that hearing the battle turned from Monsanto's favor to my favor. The report I got from my attorney was the best news I had received in a long time. I believe the new judge's wisdom and interest in the case put fear on Monsanto's lawyer's shoulders.

At this point, my confidence in God will not allow me to have any mercy upon these men who are designing the blueprint for seed control to fall into the hands of the anti-Christ.

I could make this chapter very lengthy, but because of upcoming legal proceedings, I will not speak on very many things that Monsanto has done to me, my family, my friends and business. I would like to congratulate Monsanto on their success of destroying my family and health in 2003 and the early part of 2004. I would also like to inform them that my health has been restored thanks to God. I would also like to tell them that while writing this chapter I weigh 196 pounds. In March 2004 I was down to 150 pounds. I will attribute my weight loss to fear of all the things they were doing to me and my family.

I spent many nights at other people's houses; I slept in my vehicles and spent many sleepless nights wondering if you could actually be killed for saving seed. In Spring 2004 I had a nervous breakdown because of all of the lawsuits, my destroyed family, and the other things that I have already mentioned. My mother was dying in the Spring of 2004, and my 81-year-old father was changing her diapers and being sued by Monsanto at the same time. I provided you pictures in this book of my father and mother just to let you know what Monsanto is capable of. They have no shame and seem to be unafraid of our government or the European Union and the World Trade Order.

I have read stories of other farmers in the United

States and Canada regarding the tactics Monsanto uses, and I understand what these farmers are going through. Monsanto has sued my father as a tactic to weaken me. They have no remorse of the trauma they brought on his mind while he was watching his wife of 62 years die. My mother's state of mind did not allow her in her last few months to worry of the lawsuit. It is my belief that my nervous breakdown provided me strength to fight this giant.

Monsanto did not create or speak fear into existence. All throughout Biblical history fear has been used as a great weapon. Many battles which could have been won were lost because fear was allowed to have its place in camp.

Fear has always been a very successful tool of Satan. Monsanto has simply picked up the footprints of Satan in the sand and are doing their best to follow him. He has constantly tried to control human seed using the element of fear and Monsanto uses fear to control food seed.

There are many, many stories in the Bible where fear is used in many different situations. One of the stories that comes to mind is Elijah having no fear of the 450 prophets of Baal. This is a beautiful Bible story contained in the 18th chapter of First Kings. I certainly like many verses in chapter 18 of First Kings. I greatly admire Elijah's courage in the face of 450 men whose job was to instill fear in him. I have to say I like verse 28, but it is not my favorite verse in chapter 18.

1 Kings 18:28 (KJV) And they cried aloud, and cut themselves after their manner with knives and lancets, till the blood gushed out upon them. {the blood...: Heb. poured out blood upon them}

I could very easily call verse 40 my favorite verse, but some people might not understand me being proud of the fact that Elijah killed 450 false prophets.

1 Kings 18:40 (KJV) And Elijah said unto them, Take the prophets of Baal; let not one of them escape. And they took them: and Elijah brought them down to the brook Kishon, and slew them there. {Take: or, Apprehend}

I have to tell you my favorite verse is 27 and when you read it and remember some of the things Monsanto has put me and my family and hundreds of other farm families through you will understand why I like that verse.

1 Kings 18:27 (KJV) And it came to pass at noon, that Elijah mocked them, and said, Cry aloud: for he [is] a god; either he is talking, or he is pursuing, or he is in a journey, [or] peradventure he sleepeth, and must be awaked. {Aloud: Heb. with a great voice} {he is talking: or, he meditateth} {is pursuing: Heb. hath a pursuit}

After learning about what had happened at the hearing on December 16, 2005, in the Huntsville, Alabama Federal Court, I believe that I felt a little of what Elijah felt. I wanted to tell Monsanto's lawyers "**cry aloud**" maybe your god of money, power and greed is asleep, or he failed to make the journey with you. Jump on your cell phones and call him, for it appears that he has forsaken you. God, I'll be nice now–please forgive me.

This was an enemy of Elijah, and God and fear was now beginning to come upon them. Their time was running out and they knew it. Elijah sensed this, although being a man of God he possessed a little bit of humor and enjoyed mocking them in verse 27; we see fear returning upon Elijah. In 1 Kings chapter 19 Elijah gave in to this fear.

1 Kings 19:2 (KJV) Then Jezebel sent a messenger unto Elijah, saying, So let the gods do [to

me], and more also, if I make not thy life as the life of one of them by to-morrow about this time.

1 Kings 19:4 (KJV) But he himself went a day's journey into the wilderness, and came and sat down under a juniper tree: and he requested for himself that he might die; and said, It is enough now, O Lord, take away my life; for I am not better than my fathers.

To gain understanding, I ask you to read the entire book of First Kings. The word fear is used several hundred times in the Bible. It is of no surprise to me that a company such as Monsanto uses this weapon to their advantage.

It has come to my knowledge that Monsanto also has certain issues that bring fear upon them. One of their hidden secrets is that when they succeed in litigation against a farmer, they silence him in most cases. I have noticed this to be a trend with most of the farmers in my area, especially the ones who have given Monsanto large sums of money. These farmers are silenced after these settlements are made to stop litigation against the farmer. Why is Monsanto afraid of these farmers telling their story? Monsanto on the other hand loves to boast in magazines and newspapers of what they did to these farmers.

I'm sure if Monsanto beats me in court, they'll paint my name all over the U.S. and possibly other countries. This is how they turn fear into a useful tool, forcing farmers to join their program. Understand, once you join their program you are at their mercy, whether they want to sue you or not. I know they have sent many threatening letters to many of my friends and customers. Several of my last customers had conventional seed at my place of business, yet still received threatening letters from Monsanto. This instilled fear in those customers and they would not return to my place of business.

You, the Christian reader, sit down before you read these next few lines. The first farmer in my area to run a foul with Monsanto's private seed police in 2003 was one of the area's largest farmers. He is also the Sunday School teacher at one of the larger churches in our area. He reached a settlement with Monsanto because he had saved several thousand bushels of seed and planted them in the last few years. After his settlement I called him to check on his and his wife's health and he informed me that he had settled with Monsanto but could not discuss anything about Monsanto.

I fully understand the pressure and fear Monsanto is capable of putting on a man. But you, the readers, understand this man cannot mention this happening in his Sunday School class or his church. In talking to him when he was initially attacked by Monsanto, he was asked to sign handwritten agreements by Monsanto's number one investigator who was assigned to our area. This farmer signed these handwritten letters out of fear. At one time he would call Monsanto the devil but now he has been silenced.

You, the readers, understand that the weapon of fear is in Monsanto's hands from start to finish. Almost anything you hear out of any of the thousands of farmers who have been on the battlefield with Monsanto will come before a settlement is made. Monsanto paints themselves as angels in the magazines and in their literature. The only time these "angels" flew over my house was in helicopters and airplanes that we looked at with binoculars and still could not make out any numbers on them. We actually enhanced the videos I made of certain aircraft to the point we could see the face of the pilot, yet we saw no identification numbers on the aircraft. Mitchell Scruggs has told me that Monsanto hired aircraft to be used against him in his hometown of Tupelo, Mississippi. Mr. Scruggs informed me that Monsanto could get away with many questionable tactics and I found that to be true.

As our world steadily progresses to the dreadful tribulation period, evil will steadily grow. Deception and fear tactics from men and corporations are already abounding. Some of the tactics Monsanto used against me were unbelievable. For a certain period of 2003, I'm not sure if I could leave my home without Monsanto knowing it. They had private investigators staked out at intersections to detect me on almost any road I traveled. I was traveling to Scottsboro, Alabama, one day and I recognized one of their investigator's trucks sitting beside a building with the investigator in it. I used a large vehicle to block his view of me and turned down a road that led to the rear of the store he was sitting beside. I hid my vehicle and walked up behind his vehicle, making sure he didn't detect me in his mirrors. He was half asleep and I put my hand on his arm and his expression caused me to hope he didn't have a heart condition. He had no idea I was standing inches from him. I enjoyed it, I felt like David when he cut off a piece of Saul's coat. I have trouble writing what I want to write instead of what God wants me to write. I'll try to straighten up a little and go back to the issue at hand.

2 Timothy 3:13 (KJV) But evil men and seducers shall wax worse and worse, deceiving, and being deceived.

The lead lawyers that appeared against me in Federal deposition filed suit against my elderly father and had no sympathy for him; neither did they have the nerve to deposition him. It is almost unheard of to sue someone and make no attempt to deposition that person or at least question him. I'll lay these two men right in the middle of Second Timothy 3:13. I'll congratulate them on having helped Timothy's prophesy to come true. They are beneficial to the Bible and provide proof to believers and nonbelievers that the scriptures are true.

These lawyers have made my life almost unbearable for me and my father. They just simply sued him and let him be burdened for no reason. When they read this they will be proud of their success. I ask for no sympathy but I'll fire this shot on my father's behalf. You, the lawyers, who fit the above sentence and the scripture below, read it and understand it is written in red...spoken by Jesus Christ himself. If your anger boils upon reading this scripture, understand that I didn't write it but I do feel it applies to you.

Luke 11:46 (KJV) And he said, Woe unto you also, [ye] lawyers! for ye lade men with burdens grievous to be borne, and ye yourselves touch not the burdens with one of your fingers.

I'll save you, the lawyers, who I'm speaking to the trouble of looking up the word woe and its biblical meaning and the term in which Jesus wrote it. It means "a period of great anguish." A period of great anguish is in your future.

5 CHANTS OF THE GIANT

A man, whose name I won't mention, has entered a hypothetical scenario against me in Federal Court. This man has pages of degrees and claims to be a world expert in the knowledge of world seed trade. It's easy to read his words and quickly realize he is pro-Monsanto and pro-genetically modified. As I first read his boasting of all of his degrees and all of the countries he has spoken in, fear tries to grip my mind. All of a sudden, I realize getting to face this giant seed controller could work in my favor. I'll not speak of what he said to the courts or what will be said to him during court. I'm thankful that Monsanto has sent one of the world's leading seed experts to be against me. It gives my pen confidence that I am on the right track in writing this book.

Understand that God gave seed to all human life and men such as this expert have invented a plan to control God's gift to humanity. Many of these men know exactly what they are doing and their speeches and vocabulary are groomed to deceive humanity. The anti-Christ will welcome men with this type of knowledge into his government. They will be very beneficial to him because of their accomplishments and capabilities to accomplish tighter control.

I do not know of any scripture that says men will personally know the anti-Christ before the rapture takes place. I certainly do not know him and certainly do not make any claim to know him. It is my belief that his greatest enforcement weapon will be the weapon of food shortage. The item that controls food is seed, but patents now control seed. When you line these facts in order, seed patents become the most important item to own and control food with.

Seed patents are becoming a pyramid owned by a handful of companies. These companies ration out permission to smaller companies which they can control, under what they call a licencing agreement. The large companies will remain at the top of the pyramid and retain control of the patents. Permission to use these patents can be given out and taken away at will by these large companies. There is a battle going on in the corporate world for total control of the most important patents. When the battle becomes too expensive for these companies to fight each other, I have noticed a trend. The trend is that these companies unite, giving birth to a plan that gives them joint control. The human race cannot escape these plans, whether owned jointly or by a single company. The benefit to the corporations is avoiding the costly court fights and still retaining a large share of the profits, so therefore the pyramid structure remains intact whether owned by one corporation or more than one. Of course splitting profits, means farmers paying higher prices for seed and people who "eat" pay more for food.

The anti-Christ will simply assume control of these pyramids when he acquires the courts. I do not rule out the possibility that he may already own them. With no reservation whatsoever, I know total control of seed and their patents is one of his heart's desires. I've lived my adult life in the seed business without understanding how powerful a weapon seed could be if it falls into the wrong hands. Only from this several year furnace have I come to the understanding of what is going on.

I also know within my heart that I am only scratching the surface of what is going on behind closed doors. I can see and feel things which almost have to be a revelation from God; being unworthy, it is very hard for me to make a statement that connects me directly to God. I would gladly give this cup to someone else, but there doesn't seem to be anyone else. I'm trying to shy away from words such as revelation in an attempt to not exalt myself.

Monsanto's unrelenting attacks on me continue to make me stronger. Each attack seems to initially knock me down again; after staying down a while I find myself climbing back up and a little stronger than before. With each knock down I become more determined to fight. I know when they read this book their anger will magnify and so will their attack.

As my house grows quiet and the divorce has become a much dreaded reality, spiritual weakness sets in. I can almost hear Satan laughing at me. Also, doubt begins to take its toll on me. I am unsure of whether or not I can defeat this chanting giant. I'm unsure if my family will ever be put back together on this earth. The divorce is so devastating to my mind that little room is left for survival strategy and the main courtroom war is about to start.

Sources close to Monsanto have stated that Monsanto has special plans for me; all of their threats and chants empty my spiritual bank account.

I had my youngest daughter, Emily, this week and I let my prayer life and Bible reading go. I felt the possibility of all areas of my life being destroyed. In our Sunday School lesson for this week we discussed our failing to trust God in our lives; I quickly thought of Shadrach, Meshach, and Abednego. I had to repent for my failure to trust God this week in certain areas. I have thorns that buffet me when I grow weak in the Spirit. Guess who allows those thorns to stick me . . . I do!

Monsanto has had high-level meetings where my name came up. I've heard some of the topics discussed in these meetings, and learned some of their intentions. They intend to turn the heat on the furnace to a higher degree. Monsanto, I'm sure you're reading this and wondering my source of the above statement. It is hard for me to pray for my enemies, although the Bible instructs me to. It is very hard for me to give Monsanto a token of information, but I would like to inform them that I had a gift from God which was a friend in their camp. Enough said.

Nebuchadnezzar once set up a meeting to graph high authorities into his plan. I am sure that Shadrach, Meshach, and Abednego, the three Hebrew children, knew of this meeting. I know they began to feel pressure when they learned that governors, judges, and sheriffs were attending this meeting. There is no doubt they had been watching Nebuchadnezzar building his golden image for quite some time.

Daniel 3:2 (KJV) Then Nebuchadnezzar the king sent to gather together the princes, the governors, and the captains, the judges, the treasurers, the counselors, the sheriffs, and all the rulers of the provinces, to come to the dedication of the image which Nebuchadnezzar the king had set up.

Daniel 3:4 (KJV) Then an herald cried aloud, To you it is commanded, O people, nations, and languages,

Daniel 3:5 (KJV) That at what time ye hear the sound of the cornet, flute, harp, sackbut, psaltery, dulcimer, and all kinds of music, ye fall down and worship the golden image that Nebuchadnezzar the king hath set up:

When the Herald, who was Nebuchadnezzar's spokesman, cried out I believe the three Hebrew children heard him. At that instant they knew they were on a collision course that would cause them to break a law of the land. They knew that the high officials and the mass majority of people would be against them. I'm sure they had discussions on themselves being in defiance of this new law.

I'm sure when these boys learned of the punishment for failing to worship this image, fear and doubt began to take its toll on them. After discussing and praying they decided they had rather die than to worship this new image. It was not a shock to them to find themselves in the minority, and the spotlight put on them. They answered the King with an answer of faith and doubt, but they simply told him they would not worship the new god. They told him they were going into the furnace. With faith in Daniel 3:17, they told him God would deliver them. Then in verse 18 doubt caused their statement to include the word **if.** This reveals their decision, live or die, this image was not powerful enough to receive worship from them.

Daniel 3:17 (KJV) If it be so, our God whom we serve is able to deliver us from the burning fiery furnace, and he will deliver us out of thine hand, O king.

Daniel 3:18 (KJV) But if not, be it known unto thee, O king, that we will not serve thy gods, nor worship the golden image which thou hast set up.

Nebuchadnezzar went into a rage and ordered the furnace made seven times hotter; in all likelihood, this caused the three Hebrew children to have increased doubt. That increased doubt put mental pressure on these men, but it did not cause their decision to change. We all know the three Hebrew children survived even though they had doubt. Changing from a brilliant story that included doubt, let us look at a story that excludes doubt. That is the story of a young man named David on the way to his first battlefield.

David went to the battlefield to deliver food to his brothers and check on their well-being.

1Samuel 17:17 (KJV) And Jesse said unto David his son, Take now for thy brethren an ephah of this parched [corn], and these ten loaves, and run to the camp to thy brethren;

I believe in David's mind, thoughts were already running to and fro of the bear and lion that he had already slain. I hope to some day sit down in another land and talk to David; I have a lot of questions I would like to ask him. I'd like to ask him if I'm right about some of his thoughts that aren't written down in the scriptures. I believe in his mind and spirit he knew he was being sent for some reason other than a delivery boy. As David delivered the food and heard the chants of Goliath, I do not believe he had any fear, remembering the bear and the lion he had already faced and killed. To David, Goliath was just another bear or lion. Goliath was very unfortunate having to face someone as young as David having already attained God given battlefield success. Goliath's chants put fear in Israel's army but David ignored him. The chants only caused confidence to rise up in David, causing him to feel the Spirit of the Lord.

I believe David's brothers had knowledge of him killing the bear and the lion. I do not believe they saw the connection of Goliath being just another bear or lion to David. I believe David simply told himself he had already killed two Goliaths. David saw the fear of the men of Israel when they saw and heard Goliath.

1 Samuel 17:24 (KJV) And all the men of Israel, when they saw the man, fled from him, and were sore afraid. {from...: Heb. from his face}

David possibly remembered fear trying to come upon him during his encounters with the bear and the lion; I believe David quickly remembered how fear fell in submission to the Spirit of the Lord. To David, Goliath's chants quickly had no meaning in remembrance of what the Spirit of the Lord could do. With steadfast confidence and faith, David looked past killing Goliath and asked, "What would the man who killed Goliath receive?" That's all of David's mind I'll attempt to read, but his story gives me hope against Monsanto.

Please, please, please, you the reader, do not, I repeat, do not think that I am comparing myself to David. I am not worthy to untie his shoes; on the other hand, I am able to call Monsanto a Goliath. I have noticed countless farmers, including myself, who have been struck with fear at Monsanto's chants. If I could apply 1st Samuel 17:24 and rewrite it, it would sound something like this: *And all of the farmers of the world when they see and hear Monsanto and their lawyers, they flee from them and are so afraid.*

Let God be God! He was God in the beginning, He was God in the day of David and He is still God in the day of Monsanto! Let all private investigators, lawyers, and anyone else who is associated with the enforcement of these seed patents run to the battlefield and scream your chants. Boasts of the thousands of farmers you have defeated, pattern yourself after Goliath but understand what you are a part of. Maybe some ruddy little farmer will rise up against you with the right stone in his pocket. Maybe, just maybe, there is a David out there called by the Almighty God to expose and defeat you!

There are very few volunteers for the job. The gap David stood in is a gap very few wish to stand in. Mitchell Scruggs of Tupelo, Mississippi, is standing in the gap in a greater manner than anyone I know who has been sued by Monsanto. My heart and prayers go out to him. We are studying his case and finding holes in Monsanto's armor.

It would be easy to just sit down and pray for God to fight the battle for me, but the truth of the matter is: God did not sling the stone that knocked Goliath off of his feet; he provided David courage and guidance, but David had to provide the vessel.

I've gathered some stones, but I won't reveal them until court. Who are you Monsanto that you should claim God's first gift to mankind, which is seed? I'm amazed at the magnitude of the battle that is to come with Monsanto the giant. I'm also amazed at the help that is being offered to me from people I never imagined. All of that is a positive help for me to be able to write this book.

There is a common bond between those who read this book and those who don't; you all have a soul and you all have a natural hunger for food. Your soul requires spiritual food for survival and your body requires physical food for survival. Satan's plan is to gain control of your soul using many methods available to him. His tribulation goal is to make you trade your spiritual soul for physical food. This physical food during tribulation will be purchased only if you receive his mark.

Revelations 13:17 (KJV) And that no man might buy or sell, save he that had the mark, or the name of the beast, or the number of his name.

In the spiritual discernment of what my adversary's strategy is, I sense a change taking place in some of the things my opponents are, doing are unbelievable. They are now offering immunity to many farmers who talk against me. Their initial chants in August 2003 was that they were going to sue 75 Alabama farmers. It is my belief that I may be the only farmer in Alabama to have to go to court and trial. They have made it known that they want me as a poster boy.

The hour of battle is closing to only a few months now. Their lawyers have done some things that are nothing but bribery and witness tampering. I believe their lead lawyers are not fully confident they can defeat me. They will laugh at that statement because of their strength in money, lawyers and an unbeaten record. I hate to give credit to my enemy, but they have been very successful at forcing this seed takeover into existence on a world-wide scale. Goliath was also successful until a well-guided stone brought him down in disbelief and defeat.

My weapons are not money and lawyers, I can hardly afford the one I have, but I am dependant upon the Lord for my strength. I wish I could tell of all the tactics of my adversary, but because of court I do not feel free to reveal them.

In the next few months a mind battle of the greatest proportion I've ever known will take place. I do not know what to expect upon the release of this book. If Hell itself rises up in my face, it would not surprise me.

Magazines and web sites are filled with articles pertaining to this seed issue. To my knowledge I have not read or discovered any article claiming this seed takeover to be associated with the anti-Christ. I truly believe that this is a secret that Hell itself wishes to keep. Hundreds, maybe thousands, of very intelligent men who are a part of this seed takeover will line up to call this book ludicrous. I will not place myself on the front lines of the Bible prophesy to match wits with any author of end-time events. I will place myself on the front of the seed takeover being an end-time event. In my heart I believe I am called to the front lines because of things which I know. Some of these things I have the liberty to pen down, and some of these things I do not.

My mind is in a war room and much of the battle must be fought with the wisdom of silence. That silence bothers me due to the fact I cannot put all of it in this book. The war room and the battlefield in my mind are a lonely place and I cry out to God that my enemy is too strong for me.

Psalms 18:17 (KJV) He delivered me from my strong enemy, and from them which hated me: for they were too strong for me.

6 OLD AND FULL OF DAYS

Genesis 35:29 (KJV) And Isaac gave up the ghost, and died, and was gathered unto his people, [being] ***old and full of days****: and his sons Esau and Jacob buried him.*

A dear friend of mine, who was in his 80's, passed away in November of 2004. He was a man whom I had admired since I got saved at his church in the late 70's.

He took me under his wing and guided me spiritually. This man's name was Lawson Smith and I grew to love him much. Through a twenty-five year time span I watched his health deteriorate. He was a retired farmer and through the years we shared many stories involving farming.

I visited him a few days before he died, knowing it would probably be my last time to see him alive. I sensed he was dying with the knowledge of going to a better place. He and I had grown close and shared a bond that we never talked about. That bond was his guidance in my early Christian life which helped me persevere. We knew that bond existed, yet we never discussed it.

He came to me one night in the 70's after a church service and asked me when was I going to announce my call to preach. He was the first man to say anything to me about preaching. It's been close to 30 years since the night Mr. Smith asked me that and I still do not label myself a preacher. I label myself as a speaker only.

I attended his funeral dreading the sorrow of his passing away. I was shocked when one of the preachers began to officiate over Brother Lawson's casket with a degree of joy. As I listened more carefully, I knew this preacher had no doubt that Lawson Smith was in paradise.

The preacher began to speak of Brother Lawson having died "old and full of days." He spoke of the blessings that had been bestowed upon Brother Lawson and his family members. He began to explain the words "old and full of days" as a fulfilment of an earthly life that was pleasing to God.

This funeral turned out to actually be uplifting to me. Lawson Smith alive and in death was uplifting to me. For the first time I understood what the words "old and full of days" meant.

My own father, Wayne White, is 82 years old and full of days. He is walking with a walker. His body is frail at 140 pounds and failing him. I remember 40 years ago when he was one of the strongest men in our area. He has always been strong spiritually and his spirit has grown over the years. As his physical body lessens, his spiritual walk with God increases. Monsanto sued him in August 2003 for saving seed, among many other charges. He retired from farming around 1970. Until his lawsuit was hand delivered to him, I knew of no dishonor ever leveled against him.

I would like to go into the details of the accusations against him, but I'll wait until court. I will, however, make this shocking statement, "I believe him to be the oldest farmer in the history of the world to ever be sued for saving seed."

The words "oldest" and "ever" are two far-reaching words. "Ever" is a word that can be traced back a very long way. I know this will shock some of you readers, but I believe I can trace that statement all the way back to the creation of seed on the third day of creation. I know that is a very bold and wide statement, but I truly believe it to be true. To trace the circumstances of my father all the way back to creation, Adam and Eve, and God is mind-boggling.

Until a few years ago, I had never known of anyone to get sued for saving seed until Monsanto came along. I have read many news articles of people sued by Monsanto in the late nineties up to the present. I have not read of anyone as old as my father being sued. Our research continues to prove my father to be the oldest man ever sued for saving seed, since God created seed.

Monsanto felt if they sued my father they would weaken and scare me. It actually became a blessing in disguise and an inspiration for me to write this book. Trying to understand how and why a multi-billion-dollar corporation would sue an 80 plus year old man caused me to dig for reasons.

Through research and prayer, I began to uncover an evil presence in this lawsuit. The smell of evil and deception rose from the body of Monsanto. The smell of entrapment and many other laws broken by some of Monsanto's investigators began to surface.

The silencing of farmers who payed Monsanto large sums of money began to magnify the one word question; Why? These farmers that I know, most of them Christians, have to remain quiet after they settle with Monsanto. Monsanto was quick to sue my father and now they will not even mention his name.

As I watch my father's health slip away, I notice that his mind is upon God and he has no fear of death. This lack of fear I contribute to his approximately 10,000 trips to church. I believe when God calls him I'll understand what it means for him to die "old and full of days." My father has suffered mentally and physically because of this lawsuit, but joy will come in the morning for my father.

Psalm 30:5 (KJV) For his anger [endureth but] a moment; in his favour [is] life: ***weeping may endure for a night, but joy [cometh] in the morning****. {his anger...: Heb. there is but a moment in his anger} {for a night: Heb. in the evening} {joy: Heb. singing}*

I do not know if my father will ever see a courtroom or not. That will be up to God, not Monsanto. We are certainly not afraid to walk him into court. Monsanto sued him, but they are more afraid of him than we are of them. God will choose the manner in which my father will be used.

It is an honor, not a crime, for him to be involved in God's greatest gift to humans, which is seed. I may not fully understand what is happening, but God does. I now see Monsanto suing him coming back to haunt them. I rejoice in certain things and that is certainly one of them. When my father dies he will be "old and full of days" and I will have no shame of his life.

At present, my father is suffering from a broken hip, the passing of his wife of 62 years, very little money and Monsanto's lawsuits against him. My father's name is listed in the Federal Civil Court system. We have recently noticed it being listed in a book written by the Center for Food Safety. The book is titled "Monsanto Versus U.S. Farmers." It lists my name, Wayne White, White Seed Cleaning, and White Farms Feed and Seed. You should have no trouble in believing Monsanto sued my elderly father after you view his name in an organization as large as the Center for Food Safety. I would personally like to thank the Center for Food Safety for having the courage to stand up against Monsanto and print what they printed.

Will the lawyers of Monsanto and high-ranking employees of Monsanto look across a great gulf someday and beg Wayne White for a drop of water? Will Wayne White become Monsanto's Lazarus?

Luke 16:19 (KJV) There was a certain rich man, which was clothed in purple and fine linen, and fared sumptuously every day:

20 And there was a certain beggar named Lazarus, which was laid at his gate, full of sores,

21 And desiring to be fed with the crumbs which fell from the rich man's table: moreover the dogs came and licked his sores.

22 And it came to pass, that the beggar died, and was carried by the angels into Abraham's bosom: the rich man also died, and was buried;

23 And in hell he lift up his eyes, being in torments, and seeth Abraham afar off, and Lazarus in his bosom.

24 And he cried and said, Father Abraham, have mercy on me, and send Lazarus, that he may dip the tip of his finger in water, and cool my tongue; for I am tormented in this flame.

My father does not even know that this book is being written. At this point, I've been working on it for two years. Him being sued is part of the fire that keeps this pen burning.

I certainly will not compare my father's life to David, I will however say that when my father's death comes I will compare his death to David's. My father will die at a good old age, spiritually rich and with honor; it does not matter what Monsanto says, he will die with honor!

1 Chronicles 29:28 (KJV) ***And he died in a good old age, full of days****, riches,* ***and honor****: and Solomon his son reigned in his stead.*

I am blessed to be the seed of a father who farmed the

land and produced food for tens of thousands; more than that, I am blessed by the spiritual seed he saved and sowed in my heart.

May God be with him in his last days and I'll stand in front of him and fight the giant Monsanto for him.

Monsanto, will the oldest man in the world to be sued for saving seed be the first to beat you?

Before he dies will his being "full of days" include beating you? Look what the Lord has done! Thank you, Daddy, and thank you, Lord, for allowing my father to be **old and full of days**.

Job 42:17 (KJV) So Job died, [being] old and full of days.

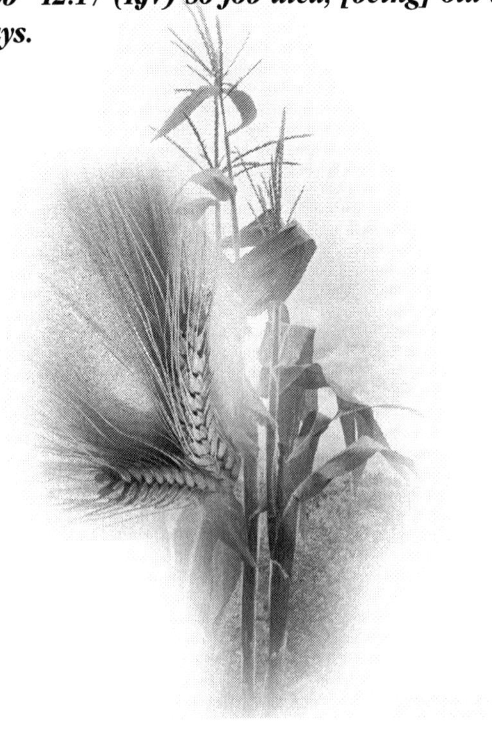

7 Putting Seed in Reverse

I was sitting in Huntsville, Alabama, a few days ago at a doctor's office. I picked up a child's Bible story book and as I began to read the author made a statement that initially insulted my spirit. He stated that the first two days of God's creation were basically boring. I began to think, "How could an author tell a child that one third of the six days of creation were boring?" Then to my amazement, the author redeemed himself and I immediately began to like him.

The author said that the first two days of creation were spent in preparation for His greatest creation, which He would create on the third day of creation. The author said that the greatest creation was seed. When I read that from the pages of a child's Bible story book, it grabbed my mind similar to when I first read Genesis 1:11,12

Genesis 1:11 (KJV) And God said, Let the earth bring forth grass, the herb yielding seed, [and] the fruit tree yielding fruit after his kind, whose seed [is] in itself, upon the earth: and it was so. {grass: Heb. tender grass}

12 And the earth brought forth grass, [and] herb yielding seed after his kind, and the tree yielding fruit, whose seed [was] in itself, after his kind: and God saw that [it was] good.

I had always thought that each day of creation was basically a day that had its own purpose. This man was able to turn simplicity into a strong purpose. I couldn't believe that as well as I know seed that I had not thought of it in the manner in which this author presented it.

The story said if you track both humans and all types of seed bearing plants and trees backwards that you would reach the same destination. He said if you began with your own genealogy, which is your lineage, and went backwards, you would end up at Adam and Eve. He also said that if you track all plant and tree seeds backwards that you would end up at Genesis 1:11,12, which is the third day of creation.

My mind constantly contains the thoughts of the importance of seed. When I make the statement that it is God's greatest creation, I am restricting that statement to pertain to food seed not human seed. There are, without a doubt, two seeds that need to be emphasized in comparison yet placed in two different categories.

I thought of a story in Nehemiah where he was restocking Jerusalem with people who could prove their lineage. In Nehemiah 7:61, he encountered a group of men which could not do that. That verse states that they could not prove their seed, whether they were of Israel.

Nehemiah 7:61 (KJV) And these [were] they which went up [also] from Telmelah, Telharesha, Cherub, Addon, and Immer: but they could not shew their father's house, nor their seed, whether they [were] of Israel. {seed: or, pedigree}

I know to you the title of this chapter "Seed in Reverse" may be a little confusing. Let us go to the last time the word "seed" is used in the Bible. Understand all of my writing and scripture use is from the KJV. In Revelation 12:17, the word "seed" is used its last time. This is where we will begin to put seed in reverse and track its lineage back to Genesis.

Let us understand there are two forces, two beings that govern this world, one of these forces is the creator, GOD. The other force is Satan, the prince of the universe. Keep your mind in remembrance we are still talking of the last time the word "seed" is used in the Bible. The last use of the word "seed" comes in the time frame of the middle of the seven years of tribulation.

Revelation 12:17 (KJV) And the dragon was wroth with the woman, and went to make war with the remnant of her seed, which keep the commandments of God, and have the testimony of Jesus Christ.

Genesis is several thousand years from Revelation, but seed has survived and made the trip, both human and food seed are still on the journey. God created them both and Satan has always tried to destroy them.

In this time frame where the word "seed" is used for its last time, Satan is very wroth. He is in a rage, his time is running out, he knows the scriptures, his ship is going down. He has set his son in power, the anti-Christ. They as a team with their decaying false prophet are swinging their last blows.

Revelation 12:12 (KJV) Therefore rejoice, [ye] heavens, and ye that dwell in them. Woe to the inhabiters of the earth and of the sea! for the devil is come down unto you, having great wrath, because he knoweth that he hath but a short time.

The unholy trinity: Satan, the False Prophet and the anti-Christ, have met behind closed doors and decided the greatest damage they can do is to destroy the woman's seed. I know in naming this woman not everyone will agree with me of whom she is. It is my belief that it is Israel and the church. I reached that decision because of the words in Revelation 12:17.

Revelation 12:17 (KJV) And the dragon was wroth with the woman, and went to make war with the remnant of her seed, which keep the commandments of God, and have the testimony of Jesus Christ.

Those words state that all people who have kept the commandments of God are to fall under the dragon's wrath. During tribulation people in the tribe of Israel and out of the tribe of Israel will suffer persecution.

In Revelation 12:2, Satan stood in the spirit world and watched Israel's virgin Mary travailing in birth and attempted to devour her child. In Revelation 12:4, this child being delivered was the seed prophesied from ancient times. Satan knew this virgin was about to give birth to Christ-the most important human seed to ever exist on earth.

Revelation 12:2 (KJV) And she being with child cried, travailing in birth, and pained to be delivered.

Revelation 12:4 (KJV) And his tail drew the third part of the stars of heaven, and did cast them to the earth: and the dragon stood before the woman which was ready to be delivered, for to devour her child as soon as it was born.

Satan failed in his attempt to devour this seed as it was born. You all know he later succeeded in seeing this ***seed*** die at the age of thirty-three. Satan's joy was short-lived; after three days this ***seed*** germinated again, came out of the ground and was caught up unto God into His throne.

Revelation 12:5 (KJV) And she brought forth a man child, who was to rule all nations with a rod of iron: and her child was caught up unto God, and [to] his throne.

Let's not forget Pharaoh in Exodus 1:22, attempting to kill a group of infant male seed as soon as they were born. In this group of seed one survived to take on the name of Moses. We all know Moses' accomplishments and his importance. Through these stories we can see Satan's pattern as he attempts to destroy important human seed.

The importance of seed, whether human or food, is no secret to Satan. It is so important to him that he believes destroying seed is the greatest thing he can do in his final hour. This should make you, understand what seed means to God, to Satan and how important it is to the human race.

Moving onto the 13th chapter of Revelation, the beast is loose upon the earth; in chapter 13, verse 11, another beast comes upon the earth. Since this book is about seed, I will not write several pages explaining the first fifteen verses of chapter 13. I will write pertaining to verses 16,17, and 18.

Verse 16 of chapter 13 is where I will return from human seed to food seed. I believe that having the ability to own patented seed such as Monsanto's, is of great importance to Satan. Once he has accomplished this, another important food seed will be in his sights. This seed is unpatented seed, commonly called conventional seed. It is already nearly impossible for a farmer to have a conventional crop not contaminated by patented seed. Through laws and regulations and the introduction of the Terminator gene, I can visualize conventional seed being eradicated.

(Conventional seed growth has decreased by my estimations in the last ten years, in America by ninety percent.) This is a rapid success rate for corporations to reap large profits. This forces a farmer to enter into an agreement with a corporation, such as Monsanto, just to obtain enough seed to farm with for one year only. Monsanto will deny the shortages of conventional seed but they already exist. At the speed in which patented seed are moving, conventional seed supplies are rapidly being depleted.

Knowing these above statements to be true allows us to step quickly into a world which can turn Revelation from prophesy to fact. Using these facts let us now transcend into a world that none of us want to endure. Let us understand Satan does not have to have any more time to be able to start his time of tribulation. I do not mean to repeat myself throughout this book, but please understand this, no seed, no food! Seed control and cloning nature may very well be how we can go from a nation of plenty to people lining up to receive a mark to buy or sell food with. To me, signing a Monsanto technology agreement is like me having an agricultural mark of the beast card in my pocket. Let's now leave one foot placed on seed control and put the other foot into the 13th chapter of Revelation.

Revelation 13:16 (KJV) And he causeth all, both small and great, rich and poor, free and bond, to receive a mark in their right hand, or in their foreheads: {to receive: Gr. to give them}

Of course this mark is the most famous mark in the world and it has not even been introduced yet. Verse 18 instructs you to have wisdom and understand this mark totals up to 666. This is the mark that will be introduced during the middle of tribulation. You must have this mark to buy and sell with; it's no secret the most sought after items will be food. Obtaining food during the last half of tribulation will consume a person's entire mind. The anti-Christ may have the power since he is nonhuman and may never have to sleep. If so, he will use his mind twenty four hours a day devising plans to make food unobtainable to those without the mark. His first thoughts will be to create food shortages and govern and control what supplies there are.

It is my belief the avenues leading up to these shortages have advanced into the final planning stage. I believe it is possible that some of these avenues have already reached the last stages of completion. That is the whole purpose of me writing this book.

I lay my life on the line in my heart-felt belief that the anti-Christ has to have total control of food seed to control food.

His agenda, even if he is a non-sleeper, is maxing out. After all, he has the task of controlling the world and defeating God. He will have great success in controlling the world which will give him some confidence that he might possibly defeat God. Of course, we the believers know his fate.

Without a doubt, Monsanto has provided near completion of his much needed seed control. Monsanto has enormous resources and many lawyers drooling to taste this money. As I speak, they are using these two resources to devastate farmers, smaller seed companies, and anyone else who does not comply with their "rules". The chapter which I titled "Be A Good Steward" is a very important chapter; it explains one of these tribulation avenues that you can actually put your hands on and read today.

I have already sat and faced some of these lawyers in a Federal deposition. I would love to write what I think of them, but I will refrain from doing so. I might expose some of our strategy for the courtroom. The anti-Christ will simply take these men's years of accomplishments with the snap of a finger. He will not only use these seed patents to create food shortages for humans, he will use these patents to create food shortages for nations. He will accomplish this by simply telling a nation's government if they don't adopt his government policies, they will not get any seed.

Monsanto states in their 2004 Technology Use Guide that you have to have a license from them to buy and sell their seed products. Monsanto's Stewardship Agreement is a perfect road map for the anti-Christ to use as a guideline for forcing nations to sign into his government. A nation will simply have to have an ID number to do commerce in the patented seed business. I feel blessed to be Monsanto's enemy.

On the inside of the front cover of Monsanto's 2004 Technology Use Guide, Monsanto starts out with the heading "A MESSAGE ABOUT SEED STEWARDSHIP". In the first paragraph Monsanto starts out by saying, "Monsanto Company is committed to enhancing grower productivity and profitability by bringing new seed technologies to market". In the last sentence of the first paragraph, Monsanto says planting seed with biotech traits requires the grower to be a good steward. The second paragraph starts with the three words "good stewardship means":

- signing a Monsanto Technology Agreement
- complying with all insect resistant management (IRM) practices of specific biotech traits as mandated by the Environmental Protection Agency (EPA)
- utilizing all seed with biotech traits for a single commercial crop
- selling harvested corn with biotech traits not yet approved by the European Union to grain handlers that confirm their acceptance or used as on farm feed

The next paragraph reads with the following language.

"If you have questions about seed stewardship or become aware of individuals utilizing biotech traits that are not representative of a good steward as noted above, please call 1-800-768-6387. Letters to report unacceptable or unauthorized behavior of individuals using biotech traits may be sent to Monsanto Trait Stewardship, 800 N. Lindbergh Blvd., C3ND, Saint Louis, MO 63167."

The next paragraph is very short, it simply says, "Information may be provided as confidential or anonymous as defined below."

"Confidential" reporting results when a person reports information to Monsanto in such a way that the reporting person's identity is known to Monsanto. Every effort will be made to protect a person's identity, but it is important to understand that a court may order Monsanto to reveal the identity of people who are known to have supplied relevant information.

"Anonymous" reporting results when a person reports information to Monsanto in such a way that the identity of the person reporting the information cannot be identified. This kind of reporting includes telephone calls, requesting anonymity in the report and unsigned letters.

Thank you for your support of seed stewardship.

We are back to Michael White writing now. The message you have just read simply tells you that you can't save seed from Monsanto's patented seed. It also encourages you to tell on your neighbor or any other person whom you have information on concerning saving Monsanto's seed.

I believe during the tribulation there will be a similar process put into place concerning Bibles and all religious material pertaining to Christ. I believe there will be hotline numbers issued by the anti-Christ and the one world government appealing for everyone to do the right thing and report anyone who believes in Christ or conducts and promotes Christianity.

Monsanto's lawyers and investigators put enormous pressure on farmers to tell on other farmers for saving seed. (I have first-hand knowledge of Joel Cape, Monsanto's lead lawyer, telling farmers that he was not after them, but he was entirely after Michael White.) He made a statement to one farmer that he didn't care how many seed the farmer had saved, he just wanted to get Michael White. He told another farmer that it was like going fishing. Sometimes you catch a big fish and sometimes you don't.

I titled this chapter "Putting Seed in Reverse" for a

purpose. Remember, God created seed in Genesis 1:11 on the third day of creation intending for seed to multiply and have seed in itself. We are now living in the day where that trend has been reversed to the point of calling a 1-800 number to tell on a farmer so Monsanto can pursue him with litigation. I'll have to say I don't believe Monsanto has any sympathy for a farmer or his family when they push litigation. I'll back that statement up with the picture of my father and mother in the photo section.

8 Burning Skin

Once again my skin is burning from the trials and tribulations that are upon me. It's Sunday morning, August 15, 2004, and I am sitting in Sunday school. Again I am noticing that all of my writing comes from the balcony of Rainsville Church of God. Hardly anyone sits in the balcony until the main sanctuary, which holds about 300 people, fills up. I tried writing on the bottom floor but there were just too many distractions. It seems I am in my own private world up here where I can listen to the singing and preaching.

The burning skin comes from the anointing to write this book and all of the possible scenarios that goes with it. Many of these things I do not have the liberty to write about just yet.

I am beginning to notice the influence and control Monsanto has in many areas. I met with my lawyer this week and a supposed "mistake" was made by Monsanto's lawyers on a farmer's name. They said I named a man that I did not. It so happened that the man they named happened to beat them a few years ago in litigation. He entered litigation against them because they sold him seed that did not have good germination. He lost a whole crop of soy beans and a lot of money. They are a very revengeful company against anyone who stands against them. These men of Monsanto are wealthy and are masterminding a takeover of the world seed and food chain. Deceit and lies appear to be a way of life for them.

Monsanto's plan is to implement this seed agreement worldwide. They have used their billions of dollars and their seed police to crush any opposition. I'll write this book to reveal this plan with the permission and command of God. This book will not come back void because it is factual, spiritual and revealing.

You, the inventors of this system, have heard criticism since you began taking away farmer's right's to save seed. You heard people cry out against genetically modified seed and especially the terminator gene. I've tried to write this book without exalting myself. I could jump on the internet and pull off high-tech information and try to impress the reader with my knowledge. That is not the leading that I am feeling from God.

Now, having no doubt that this book is commissioned by God, steps me into a spiritual arena. In this arena the devil rages and zeros in on me. I believe I've trespassed in his camp and stole a great secret from him. Being in his camp may help explain the burning skin. I'm human, I'm flesh and I may have gotten deeper in his camp than this body can withstand. I trust and pray that God is in here with me.

The devil rages now in laughter at my loss of family, business, health, sanity, and the fact that no one understands what I'm going through. If champagne doesn't evaporate in Hell, I'm sure he and his demons are having a toast. They well know the pressure they put on me, but I'm still able to say, "blessed be the name of the Lord." It seems all I have is a few days of visitation with my two daughters to draw any joy from. I carried my youngest daughter Emily to church with me today and she slept while I wrote these pages. I carried her back to Debbie and it hurt terribly to tell her bye. Everything hurts badly now; the things I used to take for granted would now be Heaven on Earth.

My mind rages out of control sometimes from the pressure of everything as the messengers line up with bad news. There are a few things, however, that keep me going. One of the greatest gifts of encouragement came from my wife, Debbie. That happened during my nervous breakdown in the Spring of 2004. She was in the emergency room with me when I asked her a question, not truly knowing what her answer would be. I was as close to death as I had ever been on that day. I asked her if she wanted me to quit fighting Monsanto? Her answer was NO, she did not want me to quit. I asked her if she thought that I could beat them, and she said, YES. A few weeks later I asked her if she remembered those questions that I had asked her and she said that she did. I asked her if she was serious that day in the hospital and she said that she was. Her believing in me was like a breath of cold air helping to cool my body and burning skin.

Many messengers lined up when this battle first began and those messengers that shocked me the most were some of my friends. Many farmers were begging me for my help and advice. I watched their pleas for help turn into anger and fear. I truly began to wonder if I had actually entered into a period of life with Job-like troubles.

Job 1:13 (KJV) And there was a day when his sons and his daughters [were] eating and drinking wine in their eldest brother's house:

14 And there came a messenger unto Job, and said, The oxen were plowing, and the asses feeding beside them:

15 And the Sabeans fell [upon them], and took them away; yea, they have slain the servants with the edge of the sword; and I only am escaped alone to tell thee.

16 While he [was] yet speaking, there came also another, and said, The fire of God is fallen from heaven, and hath burned up the sheep, and the servants, and consumed them; and I only am escaped alone to tell thee. {The fire...: or, A great fire}

17 While he [was] yet speaking, there came also another, and said, The Chadians made out three bands, and fell upon the camels, and have carried them away, yea, and slain the servants with the edge of the sword; and I only am escaped alone to tell thee. {fell: Heb. rushed}

18 While he [was] yet speaking, there came also another, and said, Thy sons and thy daughters [were] eating and drinking wine in their eldest brother's house:

It is time for me to confess to you that sometime in the Summer of 2002, after "The Dream" (chapter three), I prayed a prayer to God. This was no ordinary prayer and I wasn't sure why I would even think of praying such a prayer. As I knelt at Rainsville Church of God one Sunday night, I prayed for God to try me like Job. As I heard myself pray this prayer, I thought, "You idiot, what if God answers that," yet I meant it. Why would I sincerely pray a prayer such as that?

I did not know that I was going to be sued by a company who had billions of dollars and hundreds of lawyers. I did not know I was going to get a divorce. I did not know I was going to suffer a nervous breakdown. I did not know I was going to have to close my twenty-year-old business. I did not know I was going to write a book titled "THE 666'S ARE IN THE SEED." I did not know I would have the worry about a death threat. I did not know my mind and spirit would have to trespass into Hell to write this book. I did not know my skin would burn from the pressure of all of these circumstances.

It is now my belief that this book had to be written from these trials and tribulations. I had to go through this furnace and kill my demons, and steal secrets from those that rage against me. Little did I know this prayer would be answered and the furnace would be hotter than I could ever imagine.

Please do not take my words in the wrong manner, I'm no Job. God called Job perfect and upright. Applying the words "perfect and upright" to myself would be a terrible injustice to Job. On my best days, I'm not worthy to untie Job's shoes.

Job 1:8 (KJV) And the LORD said unto Satan, Hast thou considered my servant Job, that {there is} none like him in the earth, a perfect and an upright man, one that feareth God, and escheweth evil? {considered: Heb. set thy heart on}

The book of Job has become very special to me. I even have a book written by Charles Swindall titled "Job." Job was a hero of a different kind because of his losses. To me the most precious words coming from Job's lips are "blessed be the name of the Lord." I've tried to gain a small part of his determination and try to pattern my responses after him. My mind is only allowed to dwell on me for a short time and then it's back to the mental war room.

From inside this war room I'll tell you who sits at the conference table. On my side of the table sits God, the Spirit, myself, my lawyers, and a short supply of friends. On the other side of the table sits Satan, the false prophet, the anti-Christ, many Monsanto lawyers, many sceptics, and an unknown number of demons. In addition, some of the most hurtful people in the war room across the table are some of my old friends. These old friends have joined Monsanto out of fear of being sued themselves.

I wear the war room on my shoulders. The battle is constant. Everywhere I go I see food, restaurants, and grocery stores. I look at people and I know they have very little knowledge that God's creation of seed is what supplies all the food they are buying.

My enemies are great in number and size. I told you who was sitting in the conference room across the table. I hope and pray the judge and the USDA and certain politicians do not join this group of enemies. All of my potential witnesses are scared of Monsanto. I certainly have people praying for me, but it seems my army consists only of me and God. I probably should not have worded that sentence that way because scripture just hit me, "if God be for you who can be against you."

I wish I could talk to God audibly or that He would call me on the phone. Then again He has revealed Himself in some happenings that I cannot speak of at the moment. Some of the ammunition they plan to use against me in court, God has taken from them and given it to me. I was told from the start of this issue by a special friend that there was no money deal for me because they wanted me for a poster boy. Due to certain actions of Monsanto, I formed the opinion that they would love to put me in jail.

I believe Monsanto hoped I would lie under oath and hoped I would destroy invoices and hoped they could lay some type of trap for me that would turn this civil trial into a criminal trial. Then they would finally have human flesh in jail in a civil trial. This would be a trophy for them to scare and intimidate all farmers worldwide with. Then they could paint the farm magazines with my story and what they did to me. Understand, they buy millions of dollars worth of advertisements in these magazines. You will read very little negative talk about Monsanto in any of these magazines. They want me in their spotlight, maybe they'll get it. I pray if I'm in their spotlight it's because of this book. I pray if I have to be known for anything that I'm known for enduring the battle to write this book.

As for me, when this book is finished I'd like to go on to heaven. If it's God's will to take me, so be it. If not, I'll stay on the battlefield as long as my mind and body can endure.

I'm back in church tonight and feeling the need to pick up the pen and write. As I pass churches on the way over here, it seems fewer and fewer cars are in the parking lot. The scriptures support that; that is the way it will be in the last days. Next to all of the little country churches are agricultural fields making themselves ready for harvest. All of the fields I pass are planted from genetically modified seed.

It's a giant that is in the takeover mode and it seems that no one is noticing. If you think you are going into a common grocery store and not coming out with genetically modified food, think again. This, however, is not my battle, although it has health concerns that have not been addressed.

I apologize to you as you read this book because the events of this book were not written in order according to the months and the years of the calender. I must now give God a huge honor because He has made a way when there seemed to be no way. On December 16, 2005, a Federal Judge in Huntsville, Alabama, handed down a ruling that sent shock waves through Monsanto's "Elite Lawyers." This Judge denied summary judgment to Monsanto, clearing the way for me to have a jury trial. Experts have told me that I am one of the first out of several hundred farmers to ever get a jury trial. This gift from God through this Federal Judge was a bucket of ice water poured over my burning skin. Call me, Monsanto, if you need advice on how to deal with fear and loss of sleep. Thank you, GOD!

9 A Land With No Seed

Most people, as they look at the five word chapter title above, will have no comprehension of the seriousness of those words...should they come true. Satan, the anti-Christ, and the False Prophet know the importance of a land with no seed; God certainly knows the importance of it, for He created all seed. Monsanto knows the importance of seed and I believe that the Spirit has revealed it to me.

The battle with Monsanto is entering its third year. The vessel I walk in and the mind that drives the vessel is tired. Mental warfare is a never-ending battle; the agony of it is broken only when God intervenes. His intervention is always a welcome relief, yet always a surprise. The origin of this chapter sprouted when a good Christian friend of mine gave me 70 sheets of paper. These sheets of paper contain all Bible verses which have the word "seed" in them.

As I began to read the verses beginning with Genesis 1:11, continuing through Revelation 12:17, I had no idea inspiration for a new chapter would rise from these pages. I had studied the Strong's Concordance and the King James Version Bible and knew how many times the word "seed" was in there.

Having read more than forty verses from these sheets of paper containing the word "seed," I came upon Genesis 47:19. The 47th chapter of Genesis is where Joseph was supplying his family and the people of Egypt with food and seed. In the past year or so, I have had many Christian friends to tell me my situation compares to Joseph. Each time someone compares me to someone in the Bible I want to scream, "no!" I believe if they knew how unworthy I feel they would save me the embarrassment of comparing me to anyone in the Bible.

I was sitting at church Wednesday night, May 11, 2005, scanning the pages of scripture my friend had given me. As I read, the 19th verse of the 47th chapter of Genesis, three words grabbed my attention.

Genesis 47:19 (KJV) Wherefore shall we die before thine eyes, both we and our land? Buy us and our land for bread, and we and our lands will be servants unto Pharaoh: and give [us] seed that we may live, ***and not die****, that the lands are not desolate.*

I felt ashamed not having already discerned these three words and their importance. I read the scripture several times and my mind began to receive the leading to write this chapter. This chapter, like many others, pressed on my mind until I wrote it down.

These three words pressed on my mind so heavily in 2005 that I took off work to come home and write. The sun is shining and we are in the field farming and I'm behind as usual. This book has become more important than anything, so work has to take second place.

I almost titled this chapter with the three words, "and not die." As I read past these three words, the scripture spoke of the land not being desolate. I understood that if Joseph had not had the wisdom to save seed, these people would have died because of a desolate land.

Having studied this scripture in depth, the words "a land with no seed" stepped to the front of my mind and became the title of this chapter.

You must read several chapters preceding chapter 47 to get the real importance of verse 19 in chapter 47. Begin at least in chapter 37 and read your way up to this verse and these three words "and not die."

These were the Egyptians and Joseph's family coming to Joseph because of the famine that was upon their land. These people were begging for food. Joseph had the wisdom to know that food was only temporal and that to sustain their lives they needed seeds. It is hard for me to over-emphasize the fact that I have stated throughout this book i.e., no seed: no food.

They had land and laborers and money. Even with these necessities they realized that they would die without seed. They were offering Joseph everything but the breath in their nostrils for seed. Seed or die was their purpose for standing before Joseph. In verse 23, Joseph gave them seed and a command to sow the land.

Genesis 47:23 (KJV) Then Joseph said unto the people, Behold, I have bought you this day and your land for Pharaoh: lo, ***[here is] seed for you, and ye will sow the land.***

Notice that Joseph said in verse 23, "the land," not their land because this land now belonged to Pharaoh. The only item they got was seed. Slow down as you read verse 24 and soak it in.

Genesis 47:24 (KJV) And it shall come to pass in the increase, that ye shall give the fifth [part] unto Pharaoh, and four parts shall be your own, for seed of the field, and for your food, and for them of your households, and for food for your little ones.

Joseph was instructing them to do as we still do in America today. That is to give the land owner his share. He said to give Pharaoh one fifth of the crop of grain. Sometimes we, in America, give a fourth or a third to the land owner in our area, even in 2005, five-thousand-seven-hundred years after Joseph set the standard.

Let's notice how the people standing before Joseph responded immediately after he gave them seed and commissioned them to save seed. Read carefully and understand what they said.

Genesis 47:25 (KJV) And they said, Thou hast saved our lives: Let us find grace in the sight of my Lord and we will be Phá-raoh's servants.

There is a very important instruction given in verse 24. Joseph told them that they could keep four-fifths, or 80 percent, of what they grew. He gave them a very important command here that stands out above all of his other instructions. The most important words in this verse are the five words "for seed of the field." Their 80 percent had a dual purpose: seed and food. It was no accident that Joseph put seed in front of food. This seed of the field was his way of saying save enough seed first to plant next years' fields with. He was stressing the importance that you can eat or plant what a field produces. In other words, seed is food and food is seed. His instructions were plain, keep back an estimated amount of the grain to use for seed for the next planting.

He had given them seed for their initial crop, but it was up to them to save their own seed for their next crop. In all likelihood, at the start of the famine, these people had eaten up their seed supply for food.

I have seen financially stressed farmers sell all of their crop and fail to save any seed for the next crop. The end result of this is always having to pay more money to purchase seed from someone else the next year. My mind can't help but go to Revelation 6:6.

Revelation 6:6 (KJV) And I heard a voice in the midst of the four beasts say, A measure of wheat for a penny, and three measures of barley for a penny. [see] thou hurt not the oil and the wine.

This is a time period during tribulation when wheat is being measured out at a very high price, refer to the chapter "Seeing the End " for my explanation of this scripture.

I do not feel I need to say much more to get my point across that saving seed has always been a God-sanctioned privilege proven with scripture.

In verse 25 they were very appreciative of Joseph and awarded him the compliment of "thou hast saved our lives." They were, without a doubt, talking about seed saving their lives.

Genesis 47:25 (KJV) And they said, ***Thou hast saved our lives****: let us find grace in the sight of my lord, and we will be Pharaoh's servants.*

Listen up Monsanto lawyers, listen, this may be something you haven't thought of. Is it possible you could extend your history search in your stewardship agreement from six years to six thousand? If that is possible, you might can sue Egypt using the 47th chapter of Genesis as evidence. Joseph gave seed away. He admitted that. That would fall under your stewardship agreement that says a person can't give seed away. This is the agreement you force farmers to agree to if they purchase seed that you call yours. Also, there is sufficient evidence that the Egyptian people saved seed and so did Joseph's family. Monsanto, you may own Egypt already. My scripture research may have uncovered evidence to make you richer than you ever dreamed.

Wait one moment, Monsanto, before you sue Egypt. Think very carefully. It could be possible that in your history search extending back through the years your sin might get exposed. Maybe some of the seed you have patented could be traced back to the seed Joseph multiplied. After all, which came first, "the chicken or the egg?" Which came first Monsanto, God's seed or yours? Where do you get your seed from to patent? I'm talking about the seed before you altered it and called it "genetically modified" and got a patent on it.

As I travel through state after state and look at the beautiful crops growing, I remorse. Why do I remorse? Because I know that 90 percent of the fields I see are planted with patented seed.

Joseph's seed were not patented and neither were God's. They were created and given to be multiplied for the well-being of mankind. Don't forget the three words "and not die."

Stop the sale of patented seed today and I believe 90 percent of America's farm land would be a land with no seed. The anti-Christ will easily have the ability to stop the sale of patented seed.

If you are so naive to think you will grow a garden during tribulation, try planting marijuana where you plan to grow your garden and see if it gets detected.

Will large corporations stop the sale of seed before tribulation? Probably not until the anti-Christ gives them the order. They will, however increase the price of seed, taking the profits and using them for tighter control of seed. The excess money will be used in lawsuits and buy-outs of other seed companies. Small seed companies and people like myself are quickly becoming a thing of the past in America and the world.

To stand against this system would be foolish to me, except for the purpose of this book. This book will enlighten you to the highly visible, yet deceptive takeover of the world-wide seed supply. I could have titled this book "A Land With No Seed," but that is not the title I was given. "**The 666's are in The Seed**" is the title birthed from the travail of pain endured throughout this book. It seems I'm simply walking under the Spirit and behind Monsanto's lawyers and their tactics, penning down what I feel and see. Without the pain inflicted by these lawyers and their deceiving investigators this book would be only a few pages. I wish to thank them for their contribution.

Many very important people involved in the seed industry will read this book, and there will be very little middle ground spoken from their mouth. A very high percentage of them will call me a fool. (They will not admit to being a part of a massive seed policy that could leave a land or a world with no seed.)

Their speech against me will come from their greed for money and personal denial of having anything to do with a dangerous seed takeover. They will give many benefits and excuses for their involvement in the seed takeover. Their first denial will be that seed is not being taken over in the first place. Then they will boast of the benefits of genetically modified food.

They will call me a seed thief, a seed pirate, a fool, a criminal, and a danger to seed itself. The reason they sue me for seed multiplying is strictly money, they want it all for themselves.

They multiply from the genes of God's original seed stock. A history search on them might yield some surprising results.

Many web sites and people of high standing have attacked genetically modified food and seed. To my knowledge no one has connected them to a plan the anti-Christ will take and use to starve the world. Remember, if Joseph had not given the Egyptians seed in Genesis 47:19, they would have died. Monsanto is no Joseph.

10 Days of Deception

As I write down the words to begin this chapter, nausea seems to take control of my mind. That nausea comes from the fear that I may not accomplish my task to reveal what I see, feel and know.

Each time catastrophe comes upon the nation or world, we humans are creatures of habit. Succinctly, we all have certain places we turn to get our information as to what is happening. These places are frequented by Christians and sinners alike. Certainly, Christians turn to their prayer closets; even sinners pray in situations such as 9/11.

One of the places most frequented by Christians and sinners alike is television to listen for the world leaders' opinions. These places are no secret to Satan and the anti-Christ. Be sure Satan and the anti-Christ will have their messages hidden in these two areas. The fusion of deception commissioned by Satan and the anti-Christ has not and will not take place over night. It is already being integrated well in advance of the tribulation period.

Having to take Michael White's word on this is not sufficient. Therefore, I will ask you to go to the scriptures for proof of deception that can deceive the very elect. I'm not trying to write this book by simply copying scriptures from the Bible. There are, however, times that I have to refer to scriptures to prove my point.

The 24th chapter of Matthew scares me because it is all but fulfilled. As the disciples sat with Jesus in Matthew 24:3 (KJV): ***And as he sat upon the mount of Olives, the disciples came unto him privately, saying, Tell us, when shall***

these things be? and what [shall be] the sign of thy coming, and of the end of the world? These men, like us, were curious about the end of the world. Jesus gave them a very important instruction in verse 4 (KJV): *"And Jesus answered and said unto them, Take heed that no man deceive you."*

I would like for you to read the whole 24th chapter of Matthew. These scriptures tell us the signs of the end of the world. They tell of deception and the people who will apply this deception. There is no doubt in the religious world that modern day happenings are what the 24th chapter of Matthew is speaking of.

Verse 21 of the 24th chapter of Matthew is the verse that I fear more than any in Matthew and possibly the entire Bible: ***(KJV) "For then shall be great tribulation, such as was not since the beginning of the world to this time, no, nor ever shall be."***

In the religious world there are mainly three different opinions abut the church and tribulation. Some believe in pre-tribulation, meaning that the church will be raptured out at the beginning of the seven-year tribulation period. Some believe in mid -tribulation, which is the rapturing of the church during the middle of tribulation. Some believe that the church will endure the whole tribulation period.

As for me, I straddle the fence on this issue. I am 50 percent confident in pre-tribulation, and a 50 percent believer of mid-tribulation. I do, however, find fear in the words written in red in verse 21 that guarantees this world has never seen a type of sorrow that is to come during the great tribulation. This statement puts even Hitler's death counts and all carnage that have taken place in wars and other disasters in second place to the great tribulation.

Verse 13 of Matthew chapter 24 makes an implication that some people might wish to debate; as for me, I'll take it for the face value of what it says. I've had to apply it to my troubled life, and I must endure to the end to be saved.

Matt 24:13 (KJV) But he that shall endure unto the end, the same shall be saved.

There is an old hymn that says, "I have been told of a home far away," this song says that this home does not have any storm clouds or troubles. It says that it is a land that has been prepared since the beginning of time.

This sounds like a wonderful place, but I believe that the scripture above tells us that you have to endure till the end to reach this place. There is but one path, one door that carries you to this land of no troubles. Be very cautious as you journey to this home because the path that leads to it is narrow and not many will find it.

The narrow path has many signs along the way and it is your responsibility to read all of the signs and discern who has placed them on this path. There are only two beings allowed to place signs on this path-they are God and Satan. There is another path that is very wide and many will find and travel it. The large crowds that travel the wide path are very vocal and their instructions are loud and bountiful; their allure is spiced by promises of fun and pleasure. The only requirement these people fail to tell you about is that you have to make a payment at the end of this wide path. The payment I'm talking about is your soul and eternal damnation.

Romans 6:23 (KJV) For the wages of sin [is] death; but the gift of God [is] eternal life through Jesus Christ our Lord.

God is constantly putting warning signs on both of the paths and Satan is given the permission to call God's signs lies. You who are traveling the wide path can only exit to the narrow path when the Spirit draws you. The Spirit that draws you is not vocal so it is hard for you to tell which time is His last time to call you.

The signs on the wide path always promise you that there will be more time. Hell echoes with screams of people asking this sign why it lied to them. Your life can end at any moment; as you read these promising signs, your soul can be hurled into eternity in the duration of a second. People of all ages above accountability find the end of this path unexpectedly.

There are people in life who do not have a sufficient mind, such as the severely mentally handicapped. I believe God carries those type of people from the path of life into His kingdom. Some of the most unfortunate people in the world will wear a robe of white throughout eternity.

Let me give you an example of eternity. Should a sparrow travel to the moon and pick up a speck of moon dust and return to earth once every ten thousand years, when the sparrow has completely deposited the moon on the earth, one speck of dust every ten thousand years, eternity has hardly begun.

This book is about the takeover of seed, but I have to warn you of the two paths- one of which leads to eternal damnation and the other to eternal peace. Satan has saturated this earth and its inhabitants with deception.

I believe this seed takeover to be one of the most dangerous and massive deceptive tools satan has ever placed into existence. Though my family and I have suffered greatly during this lawsuit, if this book is the only result of this battle, it will be worth it. I count it sufficient because I went to the enemy's camp and brought back many of its pages. From many of those pages, understanding of the importance of seed will flow into the reader's mind; when that happens and you understand what has happened to seed, I pray you understand the elusive deception that is all around.

America as a whole has sat back and allowed genetically modified foods to inhabit their kitchens and their diets with very little resistance. Protesters in other countries have been very vocal and have had great success in keeping Monsanto's genetically modified seed banned from their countries. This success, however, is beginning to crumble world-wide as the United Nations is forcing countries to accept genetically-modified seed and food.

I have read a couple of books that have made it through the mine fields to publication which attack the biotech industry. The book in which you are reading now is also traveling through a mine field to reach your eyes. I certainly expect a confrontation with Monsanto, should they become aware of this book before I get it released. The spiritual confrontation has taken place since I began to write almost four years ago. I am glad that Satan doesn't have a cell phone, because I know Monsanto would immediately receive a call from him. I am sure that he would not want a picture phone anyhow, because he doesn't look like he did before God kicked him out of Heaven. I have very little freedom to put humor in this book, so I'll straighten up.

To deceive America, it is necessary to erode our dominant beliefs in many different areas of our culture. Most people think this only happens in politics. It's happening, however, in schools, the media, the entertainment industry, and many other groups in our society. The foundation of the attack which we are now experiencing is based on modern-day words such as liberal or liberalism. We can travel back in history to prophets such as Isaiah telling us that it would happen. **Isaiah 32:5-8**: ***{KJV} The vile person shall be no more called liberal, nor the churl said [to be] bountiful. 6 For the vile person will speak villany, and his heart will work iniquity,***

to practise hypocrisy, and to utter error against the LORD, to make empty the soul of the hungry, and he will cause the drink of the thirsty to fail. 7 The instruments also of the churl [are] evil: he deviseth wicked devices to destroy the poor with lying words, even when the needy speaketh right. {the needy...: or, he speaketh against the poor in judgment} 8 But the liberal deviseth liberal things; and by liberal things shall he stand. {stand: or, be established}

Liberalism is a direct descendent of a long-held secret doctrine called gnosticism. Gnosticism comes from the Greek word gnostic. The Greek word gnostic means knowledge. You will not find this word in the Bible or in the Strong's Concordance, although you can find it in a few dictionaries. You can no longer take the true meaning of gnosticism and compare it to what gnosticism represents today. Gnosticism was started by early Christian groups during the early centuries. In the past few centuries certain people claiming to possess secret knowledge have basically taken over gnosticism and perverted it into their own concept.

One well-known gnostic, Helen Blavatsky, authored a book titled "The Secret Doctrine." In this book she stated the masses are useless eaters and must be controlled by people who possess a superior knowledge. Adolph Hitler used this manner of thinking when he attempted to create a superior race and killed millions of Jewish people.

Another book written by Texe Marrs carries the title "Dark Majesty." Mr. Marrs says the world is edging forward gradually and surely towards a golden age. And when that sunlit day arrives, the masses of dull and unenlightened will have the satisfaction and benefit of being dictated to and reigned over by an illuminated order of perfect human beings.

I am sure Helen Blavastshy is now abiding in her destiny now and has become enlightened and would possibly like to rewrite her book.

One of the major areas that deception must take place in is the area of religion. Most Christian denominations belong to the National Council of Churches (NCC). The NCC was formed by Harry F. Ward in 1908, which is now made up of 36 different Christian denominations with 140,000 American congregations. The NCC belongs to the World Council of Christian Churches, which is called the WCCC.

The WCCC was founded in 1942 and one of their ultimate goals is to have a duly constituted world government and an international court administrative body with police forces having the power to enforce world-wide authority.

I believe most of the 140,000 American congregations have good intentions in serving God and do not support a one-world administrative body. Most true modern-day Christians understand that a one-world government would be taken over by the anti-Christ. Having said that, all true Christian believers know that this one-world government is going to happen because the Scriptures say it will happen.

Satan is gradually deceiving the world that this one-world government will solve all of the world's problems. Satan only sees his wishes come true because God allows man-kind influenced by Satan to build these processes. We can see these processes developing daily in various informative articles on television, newspapers, and magazines. So we have to ask ourselves a question," Are we being deceived by not recognizing a fulfillment of the Scriptures when it is so plain in the Bible and in our everyday life?" We must make the comparison and realize this is what the prophets were speaking of thousands of years ago.

Our nation stands at the door of its own destiny. I believe our nation's existence hinges on our relationship with Israel. The Lord was very specific in His explanation of what He would do for nations who bless Israel and what He would do to nations who curse Israel.

Genesis 12:1-3 *(KJV) Now the LORD had said unto Abram, Get thee out of thy country, and from thy kindred, and from thy father's house, unto a land that I will shew thee: 2 And I will make of thee a great nation, and I will bless thee, and make thy name great; and thou shalt be a blessing: 3 And I will bless them that bless thee, and curse him that curseth thee: and in thee shall all families of the earth be blessed.*

I'll leave the Sunday morning sermon type writing I just did and return to the purpose of this book. Articles are pouring into my mailbox from various organizations. As I read many articles pertaining to what is happening in the environment, I wish my book was already published. I received a phone call from a friend recently who is a vegetarian and a devout Christian, asking me where he could buy a few jars of honey. He informed me that he had always easily found honey, but couldn't find it anymore. A few days after that phone call, I received a copy of the Southeast Farm Journal. In this journal was a write-up about honey bees failing to return to their hives. Some hives contained dead bees and some hives were left totally vacant. This article said research is trying to uncover the reason for the deaths of possibly two-thirds of honey bees. A new name of a new disease was given as an explanation for the die-off. That new name simply translated into the meaning that an incurable disease equal to Aids had just hit the honey bee industry.

This type of happening does not surprise me, knowing how plants have been genetically modified to give off toxins to kill certain worms or other insects that are pests to commodity crops. My mind does not have to venture very far to wonder if these toxins are responsible for the bee die-off. My mind also ventures into the possibility that certain scientists already know what is causing this die-off, but will deceive the public with some type of explanation that has nothing to do with genetically modified plants.

We have cloned God's grasses and herbs and trees with a genetic makeup engineered by humans and turned these genetics loose in the environment–all for the love of money. Seed companies become licensed to use technology developed by large companies such as Monsanto. Monsanto invents or purchases the technologies and applies for permits from the Federal Patent Office and the USDA. I have no confidence in Monsanto being the guardian of the environment. Given their trade record, "Do you?" I have first-hand knowledge of some of their private investigators being master deceivers. I back that statement up with court records and affidavits and videos.

In ten short years we've already seen many disasters hit the food industry because of genetically modified contamination. Starlink corn made its way into the taco and tortilla chip industry a few years ago and had devastating affects on that industry. In the fall of 2006, rice producing states (Example: Arkansas) were left in chaos when shipments of conventional rice were detained by foreign countries because unapproved genetically modified rice had found its way into Arkansas's rice crop.

I was in Arkansas recently at an equipment auction and listened to farmers talk about being afraid to plant rice in 2007 because it could be quarantined again this year if just a few small GMO kernels were found among billions of kernels of conventional rice. I could probably obtain a report on Arkansas rice acreage for 2007 and I am sure it would tell me that the acreage is down from 2006. Contamination is so costly that it leads to acceptance, which leads to compliance of technology agreements produced by large companies such as Monsanto.

I recently watched a documentary on Link TV about Indian tribes in the state of Minnesota and how they were being told they couldn't harvest wild rice because some corporation had patented it. I admired one of the leaders of this tribe for calling it immoral and saying "the creator" had given it to his people for food and they had used it for thousands of years. He stated his tribe could not afford costly lawsuits. He is right, very few individuals can afford to take on Monsanto in a civil court. The court cases can cost millions of dollars and go on for years. This is a prime example of how Monsanto bullies people into submission.

11 Numbering Animals

My mind has been on the numbering of animals for two years now. I had already written several pages in 2004 on what I thought this process would consist of. I have acquired a manual published by the USDA in October 2004. I received this manual in June 2005. I am writing this chapter in June 2005. The writings that I had previously done are real close to what this manual consists of.

I have chosen to totally rewrite this chapter using the USDA manual as a guideline. I do not yet fully know how large corporations will be used in this system. Nevertheless, there is no doubt in my mind that this system will cover the smallest farmer to the largest corporation.

I would like to inform you that I write this chapter for your information in the event that you are not aware of this new world-wide system. This is not a secret or hidden procedure of the government or the USDA. It is, however, a new plan being implemented by the (USDA). Its introduction steps are very public and anyone can gather information on this subject.

There are many benefits to this new system, especially controlling the spread of animal diseases. It will also give the government an accurate account of animals that are vital to the food chain. It will give farmers a better record of animals that produce better than others. It will also give them better records in filing their taxes. That statement may scare some farmers, but the IRS will receive better information from farmers concerning the sale of livestock. This new system's short name is "NAIS." The letters NAIS stand for National Animal Identification System.

We, the United States, are not the first country to put

an animal numbering system in place. In December 2003, a cow with mad cow disease helped to intensify this program. The scientific name for mad cow disease is "Bovine Spongiform Encephalopathy."

This system, when fully operational, will be able to trace a diseased animal to its premises or farm within 48 hours. I am not attacking this new system since it is much needed because of the possibility of bio terrorism. By that statement, I mean that the threat of a terrorist attack on our food chain is certainly a possibility. Our food chain comes from rural areas that are almost impossible to safeguard. I will not give any details at the risk of giving some idiot an idea that he may not ever think of. I am sure that our Government knows much more about our vulnerability than I do. Any type of food chain contamination is no respecter of persons.

We are already living under the fear of the Asian bird flu. According to the scriptures, this world will suffer many plagues and pestilences. Chapter 24 of Matthew contains Jesus' own words telling of these events. I believe this new system could detect and stop a food chain attack much quicker in the event that it happens. We have been living in a danger zone of vulnerability without this system already being in place. I do, however, regret the fact that the information will be accessible to the anti-Christ during the tribulation. I wish that there were two switches, one that could be turned on for our benefit, and one that could be turned off so it would not benefit the anti-Christ. I know that this is impossible because once this information is acquired, it will remain in place.

I know many of you are curious to see where I am going with this chapter and why it's in the book. I promise you, I'll get there and show you the religious connection that numbering animals pertains to the end time.

All types of animals are very important walking, breathing seed. I'll temporarily touch on the Biblical importance of animals and then I'll return to the procedure of this system. The first animals God mentioned in the Bible are cattle.

Genesis 1:24 (KJV) And God said, Let the earth bring forth the living creature after his kind, cattle, and creeping thing, and beast of the earth after his kind: and it was so.

Cattle happens to be one of the largest food animals, if not the largest animal used in the world for food today. It is the first animal mentioned in the first book I've seen on the animal numbering system. This book is put out by the U.S. Department of Agriculture. The words on the front cover of the book, Premises Identification, seem to be the title of the book. It also says program aid number 1800. It says it is the first step towards a National Animal Identification System. This system is designed to totally encompass all of the United States. I believe this system, or one like it, is being applied world-wide.

The European Union, Canada and Australia have animal identification systems in place. The U.S. Department of Agriculture has made the instillation of this program one of its top priorities.

This system will give each premise or farm a permanent number. In other words, if a farm changes ownership, it will retain its permanent number.

This is one of the first agricultural pamphlets I've ever read that includes Native American tribes and their livestock. This system will also include many types of fowl: "poultry, emu's, turkeys, etc."

Because of International Trade and Commerce, this system must have total world compliance. Without world compliance, this system would be a leaking vessel. This numbering system seems to start one number short of a zillion, which is "999,999,999,999,999."

I believe this is a large enough number to number every human maintained animal in the world, that is a part of the food chain. By that statement I believe it is possible to number all animals except wildlife, which roam free and wild.

All of the information gathered in this fifteen digit numbering system will be possible to be contained in a national database.

This number will cover location, type animal, owner, and number of animals. Lot numbers will be placed on species such as poultry which are grown and moved in groups. This number will include the activation date of the premises' location and the deactivation date, should a location be taken out of production. It will tell if a farm is in production or terminated, such as sold for commercial development, houses or other methods that would take this farm out of production.

The first three numbers of the fifteen digit number will identify which world country the animal is in; example: U.S. 840 "840123456789012."

As the National Animal Identification System "NAIS" proceeds, the "AIN" will be implemented. I believe "AIN" stands for Animal Identification Number. The AINs will be distributed by local officials who either work for or are connected to the Department of Agriculture. The AINs will be attached to animals in a way that is suitable and less likely for the animal to lose it. Cattle producers will probably use ear tags. New technology gives ear tags the capability to contain "EIDs." I am already seeing the letters "EID" used in identifying a special breed of cattle. **EID** stands for **electronic identification devices**.

EIDs are already being used to identify an animal and its DNA blood type. I can see patented DNA blood beginning to move forward as patented seed have moved forward. That is a whole new arena and I lack the knowledge to enter into that arena. I can, however, visualize the patented seed policy being a blue print for patented livestock blood. Let me get back to animal identification.

The AIN will allow an individual animal to be given a lifetime number printed on some type of tag attached to and assigned to the animal. AINs and EIDs can serve the same purpose. An EID is an electronic chip that is inside or attached to a tag. This number system will tell if the premises is a producer, a handler such as a veterinary office, public or private processor, or a livestock sale barn.

This system is voluntary now, but I am of the opinion it will probably be required within the next few years.

I have outlined the plan to number animals worldwide. I had intended to write on the subject out of predictions and assumptions of how it would probably take place. I am thankful to have obtained a copy of USDA program aid 1800. I am now able to give you a more factual outline of the manner in which all animals are to be numbered.

This system is new and can certainly be modified, should future lack of control arise. It is already designed to cover such things as a child carrying an animal to competition, such as a county or state fair. That animal will soon have to be numbered to be entered into competition events.

Total knowledge of type, quantity, production, and movement of animals is covered in this system. Once this system becomes mandatory, I do not know the penalty of failure to comply or to abide by it.

I will now cross the fence from factual to my belief in what the Biblical significance of this system means.

Before I go any further, I want to emphasize that I am not connecting anyone who worked out this system to Satan or the anti-Christ. I have many good friends who work for the USDA and know many of them to be Christians. I could not tell you if 90 percent Christians designed this system or if 90 percent non-Christians designed it.

If you are offended by this chapter, I did not mean for it to be viewed that way. I fully mean for this chapter to be informative of what is taking place in the food chain. The USDA is not my enemy, nor is anyone who works for the USDA my enemy. My battle is with Satan and Monsanto.

I write this chapter as a warning to the people who miss the rapture. I hope that it helps you during that terrible time. People will leave the cities and go into the countryside to obtain food, such as wildlife, farm animals, vegetables, or anything else edible. Farm animals that have EID implants may emit radio frequencies that can easily be tracked by personnel under the anti-Christ command.

I believe that wildlife will be the first food source to be eradicated, because that is what happened during the Great Depression. The theft and slaughter of farm animals will cost many human lives. If you are storing up food and seed, you will be a prime target of hungry people. I have knowledge of a small town in Arkansas that, during the Great Depression, was robbed by farmers themselves.

For some reason, I just thought of a story an old gentleman told me around 1980. I was custom harvesting corn on his farm when I had a belt break on my combine. As we sat under a shade tree waiting for the belt to arrive from a tractor supply dealership, he shared a true story with me.

He said that during the Great Depression of the 1930's, he and two neighbor farmers had totally run out of food, except for one milk cow. They desperately needed this cow to provide milk and butter for their three families, especially for their children.

He said he and his farmer friends decided to pray desperately at his farm the evening before they were going to slaughter their one remaining cow. They were going to ask God to provide them some kind of food so they could keep their much needed cow alive. They prayed desperately that evening and then parted ways to their own homes. This man was close to 80 years old when he told me this story.

He said that the next morning he got up and went to his barn and heard a noise in one of the livestock stalls. He looked in the door where he had a salt block for his milk cow and a huge buck deer was trying to escape the stall. He simply pulled the door shut on the deer. He said that there had never been any deer seen on his farm or any other nearby farms in all of the years that he had lived there. He then went and got his neighbors that had prayed with him, and they got up into the barn loft and threw a rope over the deer's horns.

They raised the deer up and cut its throat in order to kill it. They were able to live off of this venison meat for over two weeks, then other sources of food arrived. The cow died of old age on his farm several years after that. If any sceptics don't believe God directed that deer into that barn as an answered prayer, I guess that you have that right to believe what you want.

12 Will Anyone Notice?

The times of the end have been prophesied from the days of old and many have had a history of not understanding. Noah quickly comes to my mind, preaching to the world about the upcoming flood, and yet only eight people entered the ark.

This story can be found in the 6th and the 7th chapters of Genesis. Noah spoke of the upcoming flood for more than a hundred years. The God that had repented for making man and wiped out the evil with a great flood is the same God that we serve today.

The percentage of people committing evil is less today than in the days of Noah. Only eight people were allowed on Noah's ark and the rest perished under the curse of sin. Although the amount of sin being committed today is much greater, we should take notice of God's wrath that once destroyed the earth. The reason a greater amount of sin is being committed is because several billion more people inhabit the earth today than in Noah's day. I believe the percentage of people who are conforming to sin is definitely on the increase. There is pleasure in sin and the scripture also tells us it will worsen in the last days. We should understand this: since God destroyed the world once, He will do it again. God saw Noah sufficient enough to warn the world of the flood. He now sees the prophets of old, the apostles, the disciples, and Jesus as being sufficient enough for the second destruction of the world. We have our warning, those who ignore these undeniable men who lived and walked just as Noah will place themselves in existence with the people who ignored Noah.

Satan was the roadway to the earth's destruction and he is also the one responsible for the upcoming destruction. We have the scripture-they do not tell us the day or the time, but they do tell us of the signs which are upon us. The 24th chapter of Matthew is one of those signs telling pieces of God's promises.

This chapter began bearing upon my mind as this book is about to come to an end. As I began to look for a publisher and law firm that would or could help and stand behind me, I contacted Christian lawyer groups expecting immediate help. That seemed impossible when they began to turn me down. What seemed so simple to me was not understandable by the leaders of the Christian world. We received replies to our letters mostly stating they would not be able to help us, but they would put us on their prayer list. We appreciated their prayers, but we also needed more.

I thank God that I have been given the understanding and the knowledge of what is happening in the seed world. This knowledge and understanding comes with a price to my personal life. Hundreds of sleepless nights, a destroyed family and business, and many other hardships have weakened me, but yet they have given so much strength.

This seed is a gigantic worldwide takeover trend, yet it seems to be illusive to the Christian minds of this Christian world. If no one else will step forward and try to expose this end-time biblical event, I have to say to my God, "Send me, I will go for you."

God knows my heart and my weaknesses. I believe this is why he has given me signs during this lawsuit. Many of these signs I do not have the freedom to put in print. Many of these will be saved until my day of war with Monsanto. These signs have trained me and given me the strength to increase my strength.

My adversary's lawyer, Monsanto's lead man which they have appointed to destroy me, lives or lived in New Orleans. Hurricane Katrina struck him in the fall of 2005. This man is involved in the lawsuits against me and other farmers for saving seed. He and his fellow lawyers are very powerful against farmers and I do not believe they have lost a lawsuit. This is an enemy who is too strong for me, except for God's intervention.

My lawyer and I had heard nothing from his law firm for two months after the hurricane. Finally, my lawyer talked with him and he told of his trouble as a result of this hurricane. This is a lawyer that sued my elderly father while my mother lay dying.

This lawyer told of the flood waters destroying his home and only getting to look at it from a boat. He told of his office, which was more than 30 floors high, receiving damage. He said that the windows were blown out on the floor of his firm and contaminated by the water that was picked up from the flood waters below. We are to believe that this office contained lawsuits- files of farmers which they have attacked. This is a man who seemed untouchable from many points of view. I personally believe that God struck him down.

When he reads this book, I want him to understand he is not the first person in the world to be in the path of water flowing uphill.

Joshua 3:16 (KJV) *That the waters which came down from above stood [and] rose up upon an heap very far from the city Adam, that [is] beside Zaretan: and those that came down toward the sea of the plain, [even] the salt sea, failed, [and] were cut off: and the people passed over right against Jericho.*

Monsanto seed salesmen are going through my community as I speak trying to give away free seed to farmers. This is very appealing to farmers knowing that these seed will cost them more than 100 dollars per bag if they purchased them. These salesmen, of course, do not tell these farmers of the entrapment of opening and planting one of these so-called **free**

bags of seed. When you open and plant a bag of Monsanto's seed, you automatically agree with their technology agreements. Refer to the chapter titled "Be a Good Steward" on the severity of entering into such an agreement.

These farmers, being deceived, do not notice the end result of a **free bag of seed**. This is only one of the reasons that the Spirit told me to write this chapter. A combination of preachers, teachers, lawyers and farmers tell me that they do not understand anything about the magnitude of Monsanto's worldwide takeover.

I do not level any discredit to anyone who has not noticed the worldwide magnitude of this very deceptive secret. I was at a farm supply store recently and over heard a seed salesman trying to give away a few bags of free seed. I believe that the salesman that I saw, who offered a farmer free seed knows the deception of a farmer receiving free seed. Many bags containing seed have agreements on the outside of the bag telling you if you open the bag and use the seed in it you automatically accept the seed companies requirements. I am sure that this salesman had heard my name mentioned many times, but did not know my face. I never acknowledged to him who I was, neither did he introduce himself to me.

I would have loved to cut a small piece of his clothing and mail it to him someday. I guess having read the story of David doing that to Saul made me think of this. I have a hard time controlling my flesh when I see these men of deception. My lawyer would not have been very proud of me. I guess that I am just proud that I brushed shoulders with a solider of the enemy, and he did not know who I was.

God will not allow me to do much writing like the above paragraph. He just told me to get back into line and write what He wants me to write, not what I want to write. I did not hear Him tell me to take out the above paragraph, so I will leave it in.

The seriousness of this chapter in this book shocks my mind into the real focus and the real purpose. Wake up lawyers, wake up preachers, wake up farmers, wake up politicians, and just look at what is happening. Go to the scriptures of the Word of God, prove me wrong.

Many of these happenings that I have contributed to God have placed me in a position that I have not wished to be in. Many of these happenings I do not have the liberty to put in print for you. These next few paragraphs are the hardest part yet for me to pen down.

When I read the title of this chapter, "***Will Anyone Notice?***", I have to say, "God, I notice." When the writing of this book began, I have to admit to you that I questioned myself. Now the hardest statement of this book for me to make is at hand. I have been shown by God Almighty the greatest end-time weapon currently in power that will confirm what Daniel and John prophesied. This is the requiring of a mark on the right hand or forehead for all people to buy and sell with. This is the mark that we commonly refer to as **666**. This is the mark and number which is called the *mark of the beast*. If this seed plan is not the controlling power of food shortages and where the mark of the beast gains its greatest influence, I pray that God send me to my grave. I pray for God to be my judge. All of the unbelievers and skeptics and men of knowledge and enemy lawyers, I will not bow down to you. I will bow my life and ask for the grave to God only. I have noticed and have been given these hardships and the words of this book from God, and I am thankful for it. I count myself as nothing and give God all credit and praise.

In June 2004, when I faced Monsanto's lawyers in a deposition, a very troubling spirit came over me as I walked into the room and sat down before these lawyers. I felt like I had just been placed on the front-line of a dual-purpose war. One of the war's purpose involved money; the other purpose involved spiritual wickedness. I knew who these men were and their purpose for being in front of me. I am 100 percent sure that these men fully know the whole arena of the money war. I do not know what percentage, if any, of the spiritual war that they have knowledge of.

I know these lawyers are well aware of Monsanto's intentions and ability to own the world's seed supply. As this deposition began, I quickly had to determine if the troubling spirit upon me was from God or my own flesh. With full knowledge of Monsanto's power, I quickly determined that this spirit was given to me by God. I was not customary to a spirit such as this. This spirit seemed to disallow me to have any mercy on these lawyers. I realized that they had their own free will to go forth with this whole issue. They had chosen this lifestyle and the consequences of it were theirs and not mine.

This deposition took several hours and was beneficial to me in gaining knowledge of how large and deceptive and powerful this seed takeover really is. Many things have happened since this deposition and I would like to write them down, but I do not have the liberty.

Finally, after several years in a deep valley, many things have turned to my advantage. Only the hand of God could set up certain events as this thing moves forward. Monsanto is unable to see the mighty hand of God in the spiritual secrets that me and my friends in prayer see and know. I am sure that Monsanto will laugh at this paragraph, but I welcome them to ask me about them in court.

Monsanto, I would love to write them down for you to read and I am almost persuaded to, but I cannot. I have noticed your secrets and you cannot prevent me from helping scores of others to notice. I actually do not worry or believe you have the ability to kill me before this book is published. You do not understand God's GRACE being sufficient, so don't waste your time wondering why I have no fear of you.

You are against GOD, Monsanto, so fight hard and good luck. I hope that this book helps many people to take notice of your plan, people that would have been unaware of your scheme without your attack on me and my elderly father.

The paragraph I am now writing is being written two years after the previous paragraph was written. I am in the process of correcting and finishing this book. The time for the release of this book is in the very near future. I apologize for my scattered writing being out of sequence with the four year period in which this book has been worked on. Many things have changed and I continue daily making corrections. I have to remember that much of what I have written was through the guidance of the Holy Spirit, so I cannot reorganize everything in this book just to make it earn a perfect score on a literary test.

I have recently noticed the correlation between old news and new news. Let me give you this as an example:

Show menu / ScienceDaily home page RSS feeds / Free newsletter

Source: University of California - Berkeley

Date: November 29, 2001

More on: Genetically Modified, Agriculture and Food, Cloning, Biotechnology, Botany, Biochemistry Research

This article contains several pages ranging from transgenic DNA being discovered in native Mexican corn to stating that genes from genetically modified crops that spread unintentionally can threaten the diversity of crops by crowding out our native plants.

While reading this article which was written November 29, 2001, it seemed like old news to me until I noticed one specific paragraph that grabbed my attention. That paragraph states, "The presence of the nopaline synthase terminator sequence (T-NOS) from Agrobacterium tumefasciens, another telltale sign of transgenic contamination, was detected in two of the six criollo samples tested. One criollo sample tested positive for the actual cry-1A gene of Bacillus thuringiensis (Bt), the insecticidal bacterium that kills pests feeding on corn."

(Bt) is a patented genetic gene owned by Monsanto. This is a gene that causes certain insects to die when they feed off of the plant or the pollen containing the Bt gene. When a farmer uses seed containing this gene he is required to plant parts of the field with a seed that does not contain the Bt gene. This process is called insect resistant management. It varies from planting one side of the field in a Bt hybrid and the other side in a non-Bt hybrid or planting a non-Bt hybrid around the field. There are many different patterns that can be used in fields. I have always had reservations about the so-called "refuges". These refuges are only 30 to 40 inches from the Bt hybrids. I don't know how a bug knows to eat 30 inches from where it's not suppose to eat.

After reading the above information, six years after it was written, I held in my hand a newspaper that contained a very troubling story. The newspaper is Huntsville, Alabama's "The Huntsville Times," Thursday, May 3, 2007. The story was on page A11 and starts out with a very large title "Big honeybee die-off stirs questions, fears". Source "U.S.D.A. official sees it as top threat to our food supply" by Seth Borenstein, AP Science Writer, Beltsville, Md. The first paragraph reads like this:

"Unless someone or something stops it soon, the mysterious killer that is wiping out many of the nation's honeybees could have a devastating effect on America's

dinner plate, perhaps even reducing us to a glorified bread-and-water diet."

One paragraph also sends a chilling message:

"In fact, about one-third of the human diet comes from insect-pollinated plants, and the honeybee is responsible for 80 percent of that pollination, according to the U.S. Department of Agriculture."

Since this article has come out and I've seen the major national news stations reporting on this issue, a certain element of fear has come upon me. Some of my friends and I have been looking for honeybees in clover fields and other fields that are now in bloom and I personally have not seen a single honeybee. One of my friends and his wife have searched their garden, yard, and pastures and have only seen one honeybee. I'm no scientist, but I have the right to my opinion. I am hearing that the honeybee die-off may be a result of pesticide use. I am skeptical because pesticide use in the region where I live has declined in recent years by 50 percent or more. I personally have not used an airplane to spray my crops in close to ten years. Up to the mid-1990's I used airplanes to spray pesticides almost yearly. As I understand it, the Bt gene is responsible for replacing the use of pesticides. I have to ask the question, "How many and what kind of insects does the Bt gene kill?"

The Bt gene contains something that is toxic to many insects. Basically speaking, plants with the Bt gene have their own built-in pesticides. Certain pesticides also have an affect that is toxic to many insects. If I were a scientist I would probably do what scientists do. Since I am a self-appointed scientist I have to do what my first thoughts are. Those thoughts are basically a question which is, "Is the Bt gene responsible for the die-off of our food supplying honeybees?" And I'll have to ask the question, "Will anyone notice?"

I've recently read an article published in "Seed Today" magazine, third quarter 2007. The title of the article on page 70 has a heading of "Where's the Bees?" It then states, >Billions of honeybees vanish due to mysterious "Colony collapse disorder".' The first paragraph reads:

> "What is happening to the bees? More than a quarter of the country's 2.4 million bee colonies have been lost according to an estimate from the Apiary Inspectors of America, a national group that tracks beekeeping."

> Another paragraph states:

> "If honey bees die in numbers large enough to compromise pollination, markets will respond, but may do so in ways that are detrimental to the overall economy."

> Other paragraphs read:

> "In a letter to Iowa Sen. Thomas Harkin on the Sierra Club web site, Laurel Hopwood, Chair of the Sierra Club Genetic Engineering Committee writes:

> "Highly respected scientists believe that exposure to genetically engineered crops and their plant-produced pesticides merit serious consideration as either the cause or a contributory factor to the development and spread of CCD."

> Hopwood further asserts that there are "significant holes existing in current genetic engineering technology that raise serious questions about how well we understand it and how to apply such a new emerging science.

> "If genetically engineered crops are killing honeybees, a moratorium on their planting should be considered," Hopwood concludes.

A moratorium in this situation would mean stop planting America's farmland and the world's farmland with genetically modified seed, especially the ones with the Bt gene. I am of the belief that there is not enough conventional (non-genetically modified) seed left to plant 30 percent of America's farmland. I'll quit being a self-appointed scientist now and get back to the basic writing which I am inspired to do.

In the spring of 2006 with the lawsuit gathering momentum, I was striving to break the pattern of my daily activities. I had simply grown tired of farming after having worked with my father from childhood on the farm until he gave up farming around 1970. I started my own farming business around 1975 or 1976. I decided in the spring of 2006 to try to grow some new crops which might have the potential of a greater profit than soybeans and corn had been doing for me. I had a friend who grew several hundred acres of sweet corn, watermelons, and pumpkins. I talked with him about some of the advantages and disadvantages of growing a diversity of hand-picked human consumption crops.

I decided to pursue growing approximately 100 acres of watermelons and pumpkins. I made a trip to my local farm service agency to inquire about purchasing disaster insurance on the crops. The lady that waited on me in the USDA farm service agency office informed me of a scenario that I simply did not know existed. She told me since I had no history of growing vegetable crops, I would have to pay a penalty if I planted any. She told me the penalty would be around $300 per acre. I calculated 100 acres times $300 in my mind and asked the lady if she meant a $30,000 penalty for growing 100 acres of vegetables and she said, "Yes". I returned to my friend (the vegetable grower) and told him what I had just learned. He told me that he had recently been fined approximately $30,000 for violating some type of rule in his vegetable operation.

I returned to the USDA office to see if me and my friend could grow these vegetables jointly and I was told, "No". I exhausted every avenue I could think of to grow the vegetables, only to hit a dead end. In my second or third trip to the office I was informed that the penalty could be as much as $800 per acre. You've probably already done the math on $800 times 100 acres and reached the same figure I reached, $80,000. I did some research on how this could have taken place in America and was told it was agreed upon by the USDA and the United Nations. I was told the purpose of these penalties was to let third world countries catch up with U.S. production. I did not plant any vegetables for human consumption in 2006 nor will I plant any in 2007. Please understand this has nothing to do with my lawsuit with Monsanto. This is simply a whole new arena of complex regulations regarding food production. I then contracted to grow approximately 40 acres of field peas for a seed company in Mississippi. As I was certifying my crops in the same farm office, I was informed that I would have to sign a paper that none of these peas would go for human consumption. In other words, the peas were mine, the production costs were mine, the land was either owned or rented by me, and I could not let one human being have one handful of those peas. I thought I knew the system very well, but this situation had already become law and was impacting me before I noticed.

Because of situations such as what you just read being put into place without the public and even some farmers not knowing it, I have great fear for what the near future holds for food supplies and food prices.

As I'm sitting with no notes in hand and writing simply from my mind, I feel that you would like to know what you should do to be prepared when food shortages hit America. I am almost lost for words at the scope of giving you counsel when scripture says a nation of plenty will starve to death. I would, however, advise you to start acquiring unpatented vegetable seed, and placing them in cold storage (freezers). Seed tend to hold their germination for long periods of time while frozen. If you are limited in your access to a garden spot, you can grow a lot of plants on your porch or beside your place of residence. If you live in the country and are accustomed to farming, you certainly have access to large areas that can be planted. That sentence caused an unexpected nausea to hit my mind so I must caution you to make sure you're not violating any laws that you are unaware of. I have not seen much resistance to a household growing a garden. The line that I was about to cross in 2006 was a 100 acre garden which I could not afford the penalty for growing it. I did not ask if the penalty carried any criminal charges, I just simply walked away from the idea of growing vegetables on a commercial scale.

I am struggling with advising you on what to do, other than stock piling non-perishable food. A few years ago I thought only end-time fanatics made statements like I'm making to you now. I feel like I have to be truthful to you, and the truth is that I find myself at a loss about what to do. I have access to ample, farm equipment, cultivatable land, storage, financing, and good health, yet the paths that my mind travels down have been barricaded by new government regulations and big corporation rules.

I know the dangers of seed shortage and seed control. I believe with all of my heart that God has revealed it to me. A nauseating informative anger rises to the front of my mind and gives me the confidence and courage to what I'm writing. Those who hate me for writing something that affects their hidden secrets have to take second place to what I feel God wants me to write. As I faced Mr. Scott Baucum (Monsanto's Manager Value Capture Man) in Birmingham in 2006, fear attempted to enter my mind. I looked in the future and saw multitudes of starving people in despair and chaos. I believe this man to be one of the most powerful men in the world when it comes to seed control. He stared at me with a very vile look when we met in the hallway of Birmingham, Alabama, Federal Courthouse. I looked to God that day and into the late hours of the night for my strength to do mind battle against this man. I could actually forget what he intended to do to me and offer myself as a sacrifice to expose him and his company. I'm not writing from a heart full of hatred for him and Monsanto, I'm writing from the battlefield of exposing what the scriptures assures us is going to happen.

I want myself and my elderly father to stand beside Baucum on judgment day and let God tell us which is right and which is wrong. Mr. Baucum, as you read this, I think you may have noticed what I'm talking about years before I wrote it. I think it's only fair for everyone else to be informed about what you know and do behind closed doors. I'm sure a man as nice as you does not have a problem with me informing people about a food shortage. I have enormous doubt of changing the direction of a man with your stature, enforcement power and money. I'm sure you and your lawyers will dissect this book for any possibility of bringing a lawsuit against me. I am well aware of the pressure your attorneys put on farmers to silence them during and after litigation. My most important strategy is to avoid silencing and publish this book. I am experiencing confidence and a feeling of success in God giving me the ability to complete this task. However, I'm ending this chapter now with a giant feeling of insufficiency. That feeling comes from the task of defeating complacency in a nation of plenty.

13
Desiring the Mark of the Beast

The mark of the beast has always been a controversial subject, yet we still have the freedom to discuss it and speak out against it. That freedom will one day be taken away when it actually comes to pass. This mark that I am speaking of comes from Revelation 13:18, which was the first scripture that I used in this book. Many people, including some Churches, do not even believe in the book of Revelation.

To obtain the numbers that are in the title of this book, you only have to use simple mathematics to total up the words of Revelation 13:18. The word "score" has a meaning of twenty years, so six hundred plus three twenties plus six equals **666**.

This will be a mark that will be forced upon the world to buy and sell anything with. My vocabulary does not contain the wisdom to tell you what I mean when I use the word "anything." This mark will cover all buying and selling, and I am of the belief that this mark's initial beginning will be on seed and on food. I believe all important officials in the anti-Christ government will obtain it, therefore, giving them the power to distribute it. They will make requests and force demands upon the leaders of all nations to receive this mark. Once it leaves those stations of command, it will begin to entrap common people who are in charge of seed and food. The medical field may very well be next, or the energy field which could be equal to the medical field. From those levels, it will travel into every avenue of people's lives.

This is a very hard chapter to write. It scares me,

not because of man, but because of my fear of GOD, should I misuse some words in this chapter. My eyes are closed, my mind contains nothing but a prayer to God asking Him to not let me make any mistakes and forgive me if I do. I am inside the book of Revelation deeper than my mind and body would have allowed for me to be a couple of years ago. I will come out of the mindset in which I wrote the above words, and go into easier writings. I am not allowed to do much writing as I have just done.

The word "mark" gets its name from the book of Revelation 13:16 {KJV}:

And he causeth all, both small and great, rich and poor, free and bond, to receive a mark in their right hand, or in their foreheads: {to receive: Gr. to give them}

I will now give you the verse of scripture that can give much more importance to the word "anything" than my feeble mind can.

Revelation 13:17 And that no man might buy or sell save he that had the mark, or the name of the beast, or the number of his name.

The power to introduce this mark will be given to the unholy trinity: Satan, the false prophet, and the anti-Christ. I think that the true mark of the beast will only be valid the first day of the Great Tribulation, when the anti-Christ abides in Jerusalem and proclaims himself to be GOD.

I know there are many scary items making their approach upon our technology enlightened world today. Some of the things that I have knowledge of are surgically implanted chips being placed in a person's right hand. These devices may be true replicas of the real mark, yet they do not scare me. I believe that these devices would have to be reintroduced when the real mark makes its true approach upon this world.

When the time of the mark of the beast arrives, it's decision time for the human race. Many times I'm asked how will people recognize the real mark of the beast which will doom their soul if they take it. I'm asked, "What about the people that don't know anything about it?" I will have to address those questions with scripture. God does not send people to hell without having been given the opportunity to know the truth. People destroy themselves for lack of knowledge and that is not God's fault. God grants people the ability to gain the knowledge that would keep them from perishing. He has given us the scriptures which, when studied, gives you the knowledge that this mark is coming. The one verse of scripture that I will use to assure you that everyone has access to forehand knowledge to prevent their own destruction is Hosea 4:6 {KJV}:

"My people are destroyed for lack of knowledge: because thou hast rejected knowledge, I will also reject thee, that thou shalt be no priest to me: seeing thou hast forgotten the law of thy God, I will also forget thy children."

The main point I want focus on in this scripture are the words "because thou hast rejected knowledge". I want to emphasize that people are destroyed for lack of knowledge because they have had the opportunity to receive knowledge, but rejected it. God's Spirit strives with human beings. Human beings are given the opportunity to yield to God's Spirit. If you accept that opportunity, God directs you to His holy scriptures. In those scriptures, you will find salvation through His son, Jesus. You will also find truth of future happenings. These future happenings arrived in the scriptures through God's prophets. It is easy to access and retain knowledge from the scriptures. Therefore, if you reject the Spirit, reject God, reject Jesus, reject the scriptures, then you have rejected knowledge which would have prevented your destruction.

I do not believe the authorities who have the right to distribute the mark will do it in any manner other than total deception. The anti-Christ and his men will be the most intelligent modern-day men of their time period. They will be the greatest enemy this world has ever seen. They will make Adolph Hitler look like a bunny rabbit. Their mission is to deceive and destroy the whole world. They will have the greatest success ever known. During their peak of success, without knowing the scriptures, it will look impossible to ever see this world leadership defeated.

From a human capability it will be impossible for anyone to come against the most efficient force ever seen and defeat them. The only one with the ability to defeat these beasts is the Lord Jesus Christ.

Revelation 19:20 {KJV} And the beast was taken, and with him the false prophet that wrought miracles before him, with which he deceived them that had received the mark of the beast, and them that worshipped his image. These both were cast alive into a lake of fire burning with brimstone.

I gave you the final doom of the beasts, and in hopes of you not becoming discouraged before you finish reading this chapter. This is to be the most terrible time earth has ever seen, yet it will end in only a seven-year period. The first half of the tribulation will be a deceptive, good time and then Hell itself rises to an attempt to take over all humans.

I would love to continue this chapter with such happenings as the witness in chapter 11 of the book of Revelation. Then I would tell you about the 144,000 men in Revelation 14.

Though these are great happenings that are a great

part of the defeat of the anti-Christ's government, I have to write on another matter in this chapter. This matter is the pain and suffering caused by the mark of the beast. We must get ready to face it unless we are raptured out of this world by Christ, or the grave beckons us first.

It is hard to understand the title which is applied to this chapter. This chapter has been on my mind for months now and the time has come to write of why such a terrible mark would be desired.

The desire will be caused by two large circumstances: desperation and fear. It is September 4, 2005, and New Orleans has been hit by a devastating hurricane. Many have died and many are suffering hellish conditions on earth as I write.

These people are experiencing fear and desperation that most of us Americans have never seen or experienced. This is probably one of the pestilence spoken of in Matthew 24. The sad part is Jesus said in ***Matthew 24:8 {KJV} All these [are] the beginning of sorrows***.

These sorrows will not be confined to one or two areas, but will cover the whole world.

There are people in some of these disaster areas that would take the mark right now if given the choice. That would happen because of desperation to eat and have something to drink, shelter, and their medicine.

Some people in these areas have committed suicide and many more are thinking of it. Understand, this disaster is only a week old and the last half of the tribulation will be three and a half years. It will be more than 175 weeks of troubled times, worse than this hurricane and it will be worldwide during tribulation.

As I have said during the introduction of the mark of the beast chapter, everything such as food, medication, and all other necessities to sustain human will be under the anti-Christ's government control.

There will be a method in place that places the mark of the beast in between you and what you are so desperate for, such as all the other necessities. Some people might find the title of this chapter very hard to believe or to even understand.

I have no doubt that tribulation time will get so bad that the mark of the beast will be a much sought after item.

How could something so scary and most people knowing the penalty of this mark be so desired? There are many reasons that determine the desire for the mark. As I have said, desperation and fear are the two front-runners. These two mental states of mind are partially created by Satan, the anti-Christ, the false prophet, and man. In the latter part of the tribulation, the wrath of GOD comes into play.

All of these ingredients make up a state of desperation and fear that the human mind cannot deal with for a long period of time. Police officers are committing suicide in New Orleans, LA, as I speak, over a hurricane. Understand the magnitude of the despair that is soon to come upon the evil world during the tribulation and the mark of the beast having the power to instantly cure much of the fear and desperation.

As much as I hate to say it, but the mark will be beneficial; however, it will be short lived. Its end result is death and HELL.

The scriptures tell us plainly that if you receive the Mark of the Beast, you are doomed.

Revelation 13:15 {KJV} And he had power to give life unto the image of the beast, that the image of the beast should both speak, and cause that as many as would not worship the image of the beast should be killed. {life: Gr. Breath}

Revelation 14:11 {KJV} And the smoke of their torment ascendeth up for ever and ever: and they have no rest day nor night, who worship the beast and his image and whosoever receiveth the mark of his name.

Dying for Christ during the mark's three and one half years of existence is the only antidote to overcome it. It would be much easier to give your life to Christ and miss the Great Tribulation. It would be much easier to not allow your mind to lose the knowledge of the terrible end of what the mark actually represents. It would be much easier not having to face the decision of accepting the mark, or dying. It would be much easier to not be deceived that taking the mark is the best thing that you could do during the tribulation. It is very possible that many of you reading this book could confirm the title of this chapter by being thrust into a time period that you would be a victim of "**desiring the mark of the beast**."

14
A Woman's Dream

This book was almost complete and I had no idea this chapter would be written. This chapter originated from an actual dream; I didn't have the dream, a woman had it on April 29, 2006. The woman who had the dream was named Pam. She is now Pam White, my wife. I assume you are shocked at that statement since I've left the crying stage of my divorce and have now let you know that I'm remarried.

Writing this book has spanned almost five years. A lot of things have changed and happened during these years. I know the dream that Pam had, has a very strong impact on her life. I frequently ask her to tell me about it again and I can tell it is burned into her memory. She will never forget the dream and neither will I. It will be impossible for me to totally visualize what she saw in her dream. I originally thought that listening to her tell me about it would be sufficient for me to write about it.

I have now decided to have Pam sit with me and have input in perfecting this chapter as closely as possible. It is mid-February 2007 on a Friday night as we are gathered with a typist to complete this chapter.

I feel I must start this chapter by letting you know how I first met Pam and how our relationship developed. It all started when a man that I went to high school with told me about some property for sale in Jackson County, Alabama. In March 2006, this man and I went to look at the property which was approximately one hundred acres. I had very little contact with this man over the years and had only seen him a few times since school days.

The land was about fifteen miles from my farm near Bucks Pocket State Park in the northeast corner of Alabama.

The man told me the owner of the land had died while living on the property and his family lived in Florida. He told me he found the man's body and believed he had been deceased for about three weeks. It was a very remote partial of land and I guess you can say it was in the middle of nowhere. It was completely surrounded by a forest that connects to the Bucks Pocket State Park. I do not believe I had ever been on the piece of property before we visited it that day.

We left Dutton, Alabama, and traveled the fifteen miles to the land, we took so many different roads that I lost my way. The man told me that the original owner actually painted arrows at intersections in the highways so he could find the property when he purchased it. We finally reached a gate down a long dirt road and it was locked. The man I was with had a key to the lock so we entered the property. As we drove close to a mile into the woods I was admiring the timber and could not actually visualize a house being this many miles from a paved road.

The man I was with mentioned that we should have brought a gun and that he never came to the property without a gun. He told me that people often hunted without permission on the property and many people knew the property was basically abandoned. He said he had actually caught people on the property stealing certain items. I sensed a little bit of nervousness in the man and I could tell he was bothered that he had failed to bring his gun.

We drove up to a small white house that was littered with junk of all types. It covered several acres. This issue didn't really bother me knowing that we could clean it up with a bulldozer or some other piece of equipment. We walked around the property a while and then went inside. For some unknown reason, I had a funny feeling that I didn't know the full extent of the land and the man who had lived there. The house was horrible inside, especially the room in which the owner's decomposed body was found. The man also stated to me that the house contained several dogs that had died of starvation after the owner died. The man said that no one ever checked on the owner of the property except him.

I had been in the Jackson County Rescue Squad and had experienced finding many decomposed bodies, so I had a mental picture of what was being explained to me. The man had died of natural causes as far as I know.

Although this house was only a few years old, I didn't place any monetary value on it and thought it probably needed to be burned. As we walked around inside the house, I saw many flags and symbols and books that I believe pertained to the Ku Klux Klan. I did not actually see the words "Ku Klux Klan" written on any of the material. We left the house and began to walk around the property and compare the maps we had with the property lines. I guess this sounds a little foolish but I felt like I was being watched by someone for some reason.

A few years before, I had been told about a large Ku Klux Klan rally in the Bucks Pocket area with several hundred men attending with robes and guns. I remember being told that men from several states attended this rally and actually blocked off the road going into the property. I began to wonder if this piece of property was where the Klan rally had been held. We walked around and looked at the timber and got in the truck to leave. For some unknown reason, I asked the man a question before I really thought about what I was saying. I asked him, "Is this the property where a big Klan rally was held several years before?" He looked over at me and said, "yes". You must have seen the burned cross laying back there that didn't burn up. I told him I didn't see a burned cross. He told me I walked right by it. He then told me the owner of the house allowed the rally to be held on his property and the man's family was against it, so they didn't care much for the property and wanted to sell it.

Not much was said as we drove out the narrow road leaving the small white house behind. For some reason, I was wishing I had seen the burned cross and actually wanted to go back and look at it. I didn't say anything else about it, but the thought of it just would not leave my mind. I really never understood the purpose of cross burnings at Klan rallies. Nevertheless, thoughts began to run through my mind that if I purchased that land, I would put a new cross up where the burned cross was laying. All of a sudden an idea hit me to purchase the property and turn it into a church camp and name the camp, Camp Cross, Incorporated.

The land deal proceeded for a few weeks and then fell through when one of the owner's children backed out of selling it. The same man that showed me this property told me where another place was when he found out the deal had fallen through. The other piece of property was fifty seven acres and was two miles east of the property where the Klan rally took place. I immediately went and looked at the fifty seven acre track of land and quickly saw it was well suited for a camp.

The fifty seven acre partial of land had public water and a bluff view overlooking a large rolling creek which bordered the property. It also had a very nice brick home on it and was priced $50,000 less that the first piece of property. This new piece of property had been for sale and had real estate signs lying in the carport. I really liked this piece of property, but the fact that the "for sale" sign had been taken down and placed in the carport usually means the property is sold. Neighbors told me that the signs had just been taken down and that they heard the property had sold.

I know that you're reading this chapter and getting bored with this story telling about buying a piece of property and you're trying to figure out how it applies to a woman's dream and seed. Just read a little further, it's about to come together.

I thought about waiting until the next day to contact the people who owned the fifty-seven acres. For some unknown reason, I tracked them down and found out the location where they had moved which was about fifteen miles away.

I decided to visit them that night and arrived at their house around 8:00 p.m. I asked them if their land had been sold and I was sure the answer would be "yes" because the for sale signs were down. To my no faith surprise, they said "no" that the property had not sold. I sat down at the table in their home and began to discuss the price of the land and house. They told me someone was suppose to look at the land the next morning about 8:00, so if I wanted the land, I would have to buy it that night. I didn't like the idea of negotiating a land deal in just a few minutes time.

I quickly ran a picture of the land through my mind trying to visualize a camp. The property had pasture land, barn, creek, pond, and a house, so I had to assume that was enough to start with. The devil broke into my mind while I was negotiating with these people and wanted to make sure that I was aware of something. He, the devil, wanted me to entertain the possibility that Monsanto was going to beat me in court and take everything I had, including this land if I bought it. Actually, I couldn't afford to buy this land because I couldn't even afford the legal expenses that were mounting daily in the upcoming court case which could cost hundreds of thousands of dollars. The devil assured me if I did this land deal, it would sink the ship and completely destroy me. I mentally told the devil I understood his concern about a nonprofit independent church camp named Camp Cross. I knew he would have a problem with a thirty foot tall cross being put on this property for possibly thousands of people to see while driving down the road. I told the devil that I understood that he now wished that the other cross had not been burned. After all, I wanted to give him credit for causing the idea of the camp to begin its initial stages.

I told the land owners I wanted to build a church camp on the property. To my amazement, the owner said he had always thought the land would make a good church camp and had thought of doing it himself. He would deduct $20,000 off the price if I was going to build a church camp on it. I was surprised at that knowing that in all likelihood he was going to get the full price the next morning for the property. I began to think God had a greater hand in this than I had given Him credit for. I told the land owner I would take the piece of property. I could tell his wife might not cook him breakfast the next morning for dropping the price $20,000. I then asked him what he would take for the land and the nice four wheel drive tractor which they own that was still sitting on the farm. He said if I was going to build a church camp, we would need the tractor and he would donate it plus several pieces of equipment. That statement shocked me because I valued the tractor at $15,000. I realized this man had just given me $35,000, just because the land was going to be a church camp. The man's wife jumped into the discussion and let me and him know there would be no more freebies. I never asked him, but I know he didn't get any breakfast the next morning.

The land deal was completed in May 2006. As I began to make trips to the land to start the initial stages of the development of the camp, I often saw the owners of the property. The woman learned that I was divorced and began to tell me about her daughter, who was in the process of getting a divorce. The woman kept wanting to introduce me to her daughter. I had dated three women since my divorce and none of the relationships had worked out. My life was very chaotic and the lawsuit was still consuming me. I knew my failure to have a normal relationship was my fault and had actually decided not to date anyone else until my problems were manageable.

The lady I had bought the land from was persistent that I meet her daughter, but I kept avoiding the conversation. I also found out her daughter's divorce had been appealed and wasn't final. I told the lady that I didn't want to meet her daughter in person or on the phone until her divorce was completely final. The lady showed me a picture of her daughter and I thought she was very attractive. I met Pam's daughter and she was also beautiful and had actually been Miss Teen Alabama in 1999. Pam's daughter, Heather and I spoke about my divorce and her mother's divorce and the similarities of our divorces. Neither myself nor Pam had wanted a divorce from our former spouses, so at least we had some common ground. Heather seemed to be a devout Christian.

Pam's mother kept me informed about Pam's divorce proceedings and on the day of Pam's final court date, Pam's mother called me. She informed me that Pam was officially divorced and I decided to go visit her. Pam had no idea I was coming to her house, but was expecting a phone call from me in the near future. I knew Pam had experienced a rough day in court and was emotionally drained. I bought a dozen red roses and drove to Pam's house. I thought that was a great idea until I turned up the driveway. About that time I thought, "you idiot!" What are you doing going to this woman's house with roses a few minutes after her divorce is final? I became somewhat nauseated and fear set in as I told myself I had already blown this potential relationship.

I left the roses in the truck, knocked on the door and Pam came to the door. She had a confused look on her face and reluctantly invited me in. At that moment, I couldn't have spelled my name, I was so nervous. I told her that her mom had called me and told me she was officially divorced. I told her I just wanted to come and show her my concern because I knew how stressful court could be on a person. She then invited me around the back of her home to show me some work she needed done. I thought, well she just wants me to leave. I had actually planned to not give her the roses after I became scared of my showing up without calling or notifying her. I had thought about throwing away those sixty dollar roses, then I decided, well, I didn't have anything to lose so I would give her the roses. I opened the truck door and got the roses and gave them to her. She looked at them and then just stared at me. She then showed me some work she wanted done and, needless to say, I didn't think I had done anything right that day. I actually thought I had made a fool of myself, blew any chance at dating her, spent sixty dollars on roses and would now have to do yard work for free, and then get lost.

To my surprise, she invited me in and we talked for a few hours. Her brother and his wife came over and we had snacks and the conversation went well. I visited her two nights later, on a Friday night, and we made a date for the next night. On Saturday night we traveled to Guntersville, Alabama, and ate at a seafood restaurant. We then went shopping and bought Mother's Day gifts. I took her home and then went back to my home around 11:00 p.m. I enjoyed the date and truly felt like she did also. I was afraid to tell her much about the lawsuit with Monsanto because I was afraid it would run her away. I was aware that another man was waiting for her divorce to become final and was expecting a date. I assumed he wasn't carrying the baggage of a lawsuit and she might choose to date him.

I laid down that night in peace and went to sleep. The next morning the phone rang about 7:30 a.m. I answered it and it was Pam. As she began to talk, I was shocked at what she began telling me. She said she had experienced the most scary dream that night that she may have ever experienced. Then she said she had another dream that was peaceful and it involved me. She invited me to her home for breakfast and to go to church with her. She told me when I got there she would tell me about the dreams.

There was something in her tone of voice that let me know these dreams were unusual to her. I was a little surprised, not knowing her any longer than I had, at her wanting to share a dream immediately after our first date. To be honest, I didn't know what to think. I arrived at her house and we ate breakfast and left out for church in Huntsville, Alabama. The trip would take about thirty minutes. So I drove her van for her and she began telling me about the dreams. She said the first dream was about seed and it troubled her greatly and confused her. She apologized for calling me so early and I told her that was "okay." I would have questioned her sanity, except for the fact that she mentioned the word seed in one of her dreams. My mind was racing, wanting to hear the complete details of the dream. I wondered since it pertained to seed, if it was from God, the devil, or just a coincidental, natural dream.

As Pam began to explain the dream, I just simply could not believe what I was hearing. She seemed to be much more concerned about the first dream and wanted to tell me about it first. She said the dream took place sometime around midnight. She said in the first dream she saw a huge curtain that seemed to have no end to its width or height. She said she could hear loud noises behind the curtain and was curious about what was going on behind it. She hesitated at first, but then jerked the curtain back. She saw large, evil looking rats with human faces, thousands of them, and there was seed everywhere, sacks of seed torn open, burlap sacks of seed and mounds of seed everywhere. These huge rats were playing in it, eating it, and were throwing it up in the air and catching it in their mouths like popcorn.

Pam said this fiasco seemed to go on for a long period of time. She had noticed that none of these creatures knew she was watching them. Then, all of a sudden, one of these creatures looked at Pam and began to laugh at her. Pam said all of a sudden this giant rat with a human face ran over to her and snapped its teeth at her. At this point, Pam woke up and began to pray and asked the Lord what the dream meant. A passage of scripture entered her mind--Isaiah 55:10. She wondered if she should wait until the next morning to look it up, but the more she thought about it, she felt that she had to get up and read it. After reading it, and learning that this scripture had the word "seed" in it, she wept. She then asked the Lord what this dream meant and why she had it.

Pam said she prayed for possibly an hour or more and asked God what her part was, in this dream that she did not understand. She said she thought about calling me, but decided not to because it was around 3:00 in the morning and she didn't want to wake me. Pam told me she felt fear for herself and me, but finally was able to go back to sleep.

Pam then told me about the second dream she had. In this dream, she saw me standing about twenty-five feet away from her with my back to her. She could tell it was me. She walked up behind me and put her arms around me and spoke in my ear, "I am here, I am with you, I am behind you, go forth in the name of Jesus, you mighty man of valor." Pam said I stood motionless in the dream and did not say anything to her. She then said she woke up and realized she was suppose to support me in some manner that she didn't fully understand. She said she didn't go back to sleep at all and waited about calling me until she was sure she wouldn't wake me up.

As I told you earlier in this chapter, I had to get Pam to sit with me to write her dreams exactly like she experienced them. I have a problem with the words "you mighty man of valor". I did not want to put these words in this book because I have tried to write it without exalting myself, and I would not have used the word "valor" except Pam has constantly told me it's the exact word she said in the dream.

As we drove on towards church that morning, in Huntsville, her dreams were weighing heavy on my mind. To me it was unbelievable at the deep meaning her dreams revealed. It was also unbelievable to me how simplified the meaning was when I visualized what Pam saw in her dreams.

Pam asked me if the dreams meant anything to me and if so, what was the meaning. Please do not think that I am boasting of any prophetical power to interpret dreams. I do, however, have to tell you it was simple for me to interpret Pam's dreams.

Here is the meaning of the first dream: The giant curtain represents this whole seed takeover being done behind closed doors without the masses of the world knowing about it. It was no coincidence that God used rats to depict seed being destroyed. As all seedmen know, rats are a huge problem in warehouses where seed is stored. The fact I just stated is the first part of the rat's two-fold meaning. Pam stated that the rats in her dream also looked demonic. The demonic implication emphasizes the second requirement for these rats to fulfill their two-fold duty. The second part of this two-fold duty has a demonic implication of which satan is the orchestrator. The reason Pam understood these rats to be demonic is because this takeover of seed will one day come under the demonic control of the anti-Christ.

The playing in the seed and laughing means that these demonic creatures have a surplus of seed which they can afford to waste. These rats are laughing because they feel they are unnoticed and unheard behind this giant curtain. I pray that this book pulls the curtain back permanently for the world to see what is going on behind the curtain that Pam saw in her dream. My whole purpose of writing this book is to pull that curtain back and prop it open permanently for everyone else to see. Actually, I hope this book burns up the curtain completely.

In Pam's dream, she saw burlap bags of seed being destroyed. Burlap is an old type of cloth that use to be used abundantly in the seed business. Burlap has been almost completely replaced with paper, poly, or plastic bags. Burlap bags represent the old varieties of un-patented seed which have been depleted in the last ten years by approximately ninety percent. The human faces on the demonic rats represent the people who are in charge of seed control and the destruction of un-patented public variety seed. Monsanto's lead lawyer, Joel Cape, helped to authenticate Pam's dream in a speech at the Arkansas Seed Growers meeting in Brinkley, Arkansas. His speech took place six weeks before Pam had her dreams. He was quoted in the Southeast Farm Press on Wednesday, March 8, 2006, making statements pertaining to older varieties of seed that could be saved. Here is a paragraph from his speech:

"It's important to pay attention to what version of the law a particular variety is protected under. Those protected from 1970 through around 1993 can still be saved and sold. How many of those varieties remain available, I'm not sure. But certificates post-1994 prevent saved seed from being sold."

If I agree with Joel Cape on anything, it is his statement of "I'm not sure" when he was talking about how many of the older varieties of seed are left for the public to use for planting or planting crops. Varieties of seed that were common in my area five years ago are almost unattainable now.

Returning to Pam's dream, she stated these giant rats had normal looking human faces. I would have loved to have had the opportunity to personally see what Pam saw in her dream and had the opportunity to look at the large rat that came over to her and snapped its teeth. I believe that was symbolic of the demonic rat with the human face recognizing Pam and connecting her to me. I'll always wonder if the face that rat had resembled Joel Cape, who was Monsanto's lead lawyer against me. I believe this rat's action was actually an attempt to scare Pam away from me. By the grace of God, it had a different effect and drew Pam close to me. She has been at peace with this dream ever since I told her the meaning of it and let her know about this book.

The meaning of the second dream is very easy for me to interpret, due to the fact that I had been praying for God to give me a woman that would stand behind me and support me. For the last four years I have known that this task would not be easy and it would take a special woman to stand behind me. God gave Pam this dream to give her strength to be able to stand behind me. She has been a very important force, thus far, and has certainly made my walk through this minefield much easier. I have her there to support me and she always supports my decisions. The reason I did not say anything to Pam in her second dream or even acknowledge her being there is this, "I have been looking into the future and I do not know what that future consists of." Nevertheless, I have already made up my mind to walk into that unknown future--trusting in God and never looking back. I have progressed at a much faster pace since I met and married Pam. It is unbelievable how much strength I have gained from her dreams. This is a type of strength that Monsanto has no knowledge of and can do nothing about, even when I openly tell them in the pages of this book.

Monsanto will not understand this chapter. They will probably laugh at it and call me an idiot. With all their money, lawyers and intelligence, they still do not have the ability to invalidate Pam's dreams. I believe I have experienced the eating of a crumb that has fallen from Daniel's table. I do not mean that statement to be boastful, I simply mean, that I have experienced the interpretation of a dream and the certainty and peace of mind that I have interpreted it correctly. I believe I got to feel just a tiny drop of water from Daniel's river and his ability to interpret the present day situation with ease. I have no doubt that God gave me the ability to interpret Pam's dreams correctly.

After that Sunday morning trip to church following our first date, mine and Pam's relationship became welded. Her dream gave us overnight assurance that God had put us together.

Pam and I became engaged a couple of months after her dreams. The court proceedings was completed about four days before we got married. Pam constantly prayed for me to make the right decision during the mediation. I certainly was aware of the stress a lengthy trial would put on a new marriage. Nevertheless, I can truthfully say that my decision to end this court process was based on the painting and the writing on the wall. I certainly did not want to start a new marriage with the type of pressure this court case would have presented. I was, however, prepared to sacrifice my personal life to do God's will. Much of my strategy in the courtroom was secretly designed to keep Monsanto unaware of this book. It was also designed to escape being silenced if Monsanto was already aware of this book. The book was never mentioned in the courtroom, but my lawyers aggressively pursued its protection.

As I sit here writing, I'm also aware that this book has the potential to put severe stress on mine and Pam's marriage. I guess that's all the negative writing I need to do. I'll simply trust God to handle the future if it becomes problematic. New doors are beginning to open with this book and what lies behind those doors is unknown. Pam is very strong and supports me with the publishing of this book. Her support seems to come natural to her because of how real her dreams were to her.

I believe countless millions of people have gotten direction from God-given dreams. Dreams are very prevalent in the Bible in giving people directions in many different manners. There are numerous dreams in the Bible which gave people God-given direction. There are also many visions in the Bible and I believe there also is the possibility of a dream/vision combination.

15 The Conference Room of Hell

Isaiah 14:12 How art thou fallen from heaven, O Lucifer, son of the morning_ [how] art thou cut down to the ground, which didst weaken the nations_ {O Lucifer: or, O day star} 13 For thou hast said in thine heart, I will ascend into heaven, I will exalt my throne above the stars of God: I will sit also upon the mount of the congregation, in the sides of the north: 14 I will ascend above the heights of the clouds; I will be like the most High.

To understand what is going on in this world, we must understand what is going on in other worlds. Those other two worlds are God's-world and Satan's world. We must understand that they were both created for a purpose. Hell was created for satan and his angels. Heaven was created for God and His angels and His people.

We reside in and live in our world, which is earth. We must journey back in time to understand the present. The current happenings in Satan's conference room are a result of him being cast from Heaven, which is described in Isaiah, who tells us of that event countless years ago. Let us look at the different lives satan has lived and the deceitfulness of satan, so that we can understand his true personality. What he would have you to understand about him will always be the opposite of his true intentions and mindset.

His mind is revealed in the scriptures for us to understand. God has given us His word for many purposes, and to understand Satan is one of the main purposes of the Bible.

Satan's life history is contained in the Bible, his past, present, and future intentions are contained in this precious book. Let us do a history search on satan to understand what is going on in his modern day mind. My history search on satan is closely compared to the manner in which Monsanto does a history search on farmers. That is why I have no doubt Satan's conferences contain discussion of the world's seed takeover, which Monsanto has laid on a golden platter for him and the anti-Christ to obtain.

I have personally chosen the King James Version Bible to get my understanding. I truly believe that is the Bible God wants me to use to write this book. "I'll not leave seed out of a chapter of this book, especially this chapter when it is being closely watched and discussed right now by Satan and his planners." This chapter is for us to put Satan in our field of vision and read his history, beginning with his origin, which is his birth certificate.

The first thing we need to know about Satan is that he did not start in the garden of Eden, and his first actions was not the temptation of Eve. I would like to give you evidence on Satan's history by using the words of a man whom satan himself recognized, and actually speaks truthfully to. I do not make a mistake by saying that satan can actually tell the truth. However, satan is only truthful to God and Jesus, not to humans.

Jesus knows the full history of satan, and I love one of those pieces of history that Jesus shares with us in his word. *Luke 10:18 (KJV) And he said unto them, **I beheld Satan as lightning fall from heaven.*** In writing this chapter I feel blessed to have Jesus backing up my writing. I chose to use this scripture, but do not confuse it as the beginning of satan. Satan has a very long and complex history. At the time that Jesus saw this happening, satan had already been created by God. I believe it is the words of some of the greatest people in the Bible that I can possibly find to help me write this chapter. I believe that it is impossible for me or anyone else to put a time period on Satan's creation.

The three people whose words that I have chosen to use are Jesus, Isaiah, and Ezekiel. Jesus was a witness to Satan's expulsion from Heaven. Isaiah certainly knew satan's past and future, that is why I used Isaiah's words to start this chapter. I believe that you should turn back to the beginning of this chapter and read Isaiah's scripture again.

Ezekiel is the person whom I have chosen to push us back into satan's history as far as we can possibly go. These scriptures speak of a time, one that was held countless years before Christ beheld satan as lightning fall from Heaven.

Ezekiel 28:13 (KJV) Thou hast been in Eden the garden of God; every precious stone [was] thy covering, the sardius, topaz, and the diamond, the beryl, the onyx, and the jasper, the sapphire, the emerald, and the carbuncle, and gold: the workmanship of thy tabrets and of thy pipes was prepared in thee in the day that thou wast created. {sardius: or, ruby} {beryl: or, chrysolite} {emerald: or, chrysoprase} 14 Thou [art] the anointed cherub that covereth; and I have set thee [so]: thou wast upon the holy mountain of God; thou hast walked up and down in the midst of the stones of fire. 15 Thou [wast] perfect in thy ways from the day that thou wast created, till iniquity was found in thee.

In the fifteenth verse Ezekiel spoke of the day that satan was created. This day carries us as far back as we need to go to begin our journey from Satan's birth to his present day conference room. Now that we have Jesus and two of the greatest prophets that have ever lived explaining Satan's beginning and his history, let us sneak into his conference room and steal some of his secrets.

I have no doubt as Satan plans for the tribulation period he is constantly aware of having lost the first war he fought with God. He was disgraced, wounded, and crippled. His wisdom is embarrassed, and he is scared. He is a demonic leader living with shame. Nevertheless, the beings or people or demons that sit in this room with Satan have full confidence in him. He does not show them any weakness whatsoever.

This is not Michael White writing this chapter, but it is the Spirit of God, using worthy men's writings and understanding. So I have asked the Spirit to secretly record the talk that is going on in the conference room of Hell. I have asked the Spirit to reveal those secrets in the pages of this chapter.

This chapter is designed to step into the war planning room of Hell and listen, understand and write down the intentions of satan, the anti-Christ, and the false prophet's plans to defeat God. I genuinely believe that *they* truly believe they can defeat God. Satan is the only one of the three that has entertained doubt. He has allowed his ambition to deceive his own self again and has the ability to ignore his doubt.

In all wars it is important to know the strengths and weaknesses of your enemy. We should always remember that satan has already been defeated, and will be defeated in the future. With wisdom, however, we should understand satan has a window of opportunity to operate in, between his first and final defeat. Unfortunately for us, we are living in his window of opportunity. We are, however, very fortunate to have a risen Savior guide us in defeating satan. I do not want to be out in front of Christ our Savior. I believe wisdom tells us to let Christ be in front of us. We would be naive to think that satan is not studying the weaknesses of the modern day human race. Satan shares common ground with us in the fact that neither of us possess knowledge of when the rapture will take place.

The rapture of the Church will instantly trigger the alarm in satan's world. He and his government will instantly be cast from the conference room to the battlefield. He knows the scriptures, he knows his time is short - *Revelation 12:12 (KJV) Therefore rejoice, [ye] heavens, and ye that dwell in them. Woe to the inhabiters of the earth and of the sea_for the devil is come down unto you, having great wrath,* ***because he knoweth that he hath but a short time.***

As a Christian people in the past few years we have seen that our time is short. I believe that this is the Holy Spirit giving us that ability. The Holy Spirit is our surveillance and our intelligence source freely given to us by God. Satan does not have the power to intercept messages sent by the Holy Spirit to Christians. He does have the power to read Christians' reactions after they have received the messages from the Holy Spirit. Believing this to be true, we will begin to understand why his conference room goes nonstop. He will always feel insecure because of his first defeat. He himself will deceive the anti-Christ and the false prophet. If they read this book, they will laugh at this statement, so I have no fear of unintentionally helping them. To understand that he is looking for our weaknesses, we certainly need to know our own weaknesses. The greatest weakness that could be cast upon the world as a whole is hunger.

There are many weaknesses that are already upon the human race, our thirst for oil, religions of false doctrines, and our dependence on medications to cure sicknesses and disease are only a few of our larger weaknesses. The largest weakness that the world as a whole will suffer from, either before or during the tribulation, is a shortage of food.

In the twenty-forth chapter of Matthew in verse seven,

Christ speaks of a famine as a certain end-time event. In Matthew 24:8 He says that these are the beginning of sorrows. In verse nine, He speaks of Christians being killed in the last days. Sometimes when I read verse nine, I wonder if that scripture includes me? I do not know how this book will effect Christians or non-Christians. I do know the comments I've written in this book backed up by factual events in scriptures will be hated by the demonic world.

I actually believe if the anti-Christ is alive on this earth, he will read this book and hate me. I would feel blessed if my name and this book gets discussed in the conference room of hell. I can truthfully make this statement because of the many battles I have fought that have given me the will power to die, if need be, just to write this book.

The title of this book, **"THE 666'S ARE IN THE SEED"** was not an easy title to deal with. The title was confirmed when I felt an invoice had been stolen from my place of business, I believe this invoice to contain number **999**. I don't have to explain what the number **999** looks like upside-down. That particular happening gave me the confidence to go ahead and title this book as I had initially been led to.

Satan's conference room certainly has countless large plans in place that are being prepared for the introduction upon the human race. Many of his largest plans such as wars, false prophets, evil government leaders, immorality, and bountiful iniquity are just a few of his larger weapons. These are very noticeable weapons, yet the world seed takeover, which will eventually cause world hunger, is the largest of them all. If my perception and belief of this is not true, I ask God to strike me dead. I wish to thank Monsanto for their attack upon me and my elderly father because they have helped expose Satan's intentions. Even though I give them thanks, I still wish to remain enemies with them. I'm sure Monsanto's name is being discussed in Satan's conference room as a friend, and not an enemy.

It is amazing how Isaiah, whose scriptures I used at the beginning of this chapter, takes us in only four verses of Satan's exit from Heaven to his prominent residence in Hell. In between satan being cast out of Heaven and his end, which is still yet to come, he has spent his time going to and fro planning for the end.

Satan made attempts to kill many of the Old Testament prophets before they could get their words penned down on paper for us to read. We should admire and seek to understand these men's contribution to our modern day world. Isaiah's writing about satan were not void words, yet words that were meant to be understood by future generations, including us.

Isaiah, Ezekiel, Daniel, and John the Revelator are some of the main prophets that had visions of the future, which this earth is yet to endure.

Sitting in the conference of hell satan presents himself as the angel of light. His board members and the CEO of his board, which is the anti-Christ, are presenting themselves also as angels of *light. II Corinthians (KJV) 14 And no marvel; for Satan himself is transformed into* ***an angel of light****. 15 Therefore [it is] no great thing if his ministers also be transformed as the ministers of righteousness; whose end shall be according to their works.*

In all likelihood, the anti-Christ stands in front of a mirror grooming himself for his day, which is soon to come. Without a doubt, he has on one of the finest suits that money can buy. His hair and his facial features are in perfect detail. He adjusts his tie, and listens closely as satan and the false prophet brag about his appearance and commend him on his never before seen ability to deceive the whole world. They tell him that he will be the first to ever dwell upon the earth, and to make all people worship him and the power to kill the ones that don't.

Revelation 13:7 (KJV) And it was given unto him to make war with the saints, and to ***overcome*** *them: and* ***power*** *was given him over all kindred, and tongues, and nations. 8 And all that dwell upon the earth shall* ***worship*** *him, whose names are not written in the book of life of the Lamb slain from the foundation of the world.*

The false prophet, who is actually a beast transformed into a man who has just as much power and deceptive appeal as the anti-Christ, gives the anti-Christ words of comfort and pledges his support.

Revelation 13:11 (KJV) And I beheld another beast coming up out of the earth; and he had two horns like a lamb, and he spake as a dragon. ***12 And he exerciseth all the power of the first beast*** *before him, and causeth the earth and them which dwell therein to worship the first beast, whose deadly wound was healed.*

The false prophet understands that there may be a possibility that the anti-Christ worries about his deadly wounds and his premature death. The false prophet does not mention any scripture. However, he guarantees him that he and satan have the power to raise him from the dead. The false prophet tells him that this short period of death is beneficial because his resurrection will be without measure, causing countless people to worship him. The false prophet tells him that this event alone with the false prophet's own ability to perform miracles in the sight of men has never before been seen on the earth.

Revelation 13:13 (KJV) And he doeth great wonders, so that he maketh fire come down from heaven on the earth in the sight of men, 14 And deceiveth them that dwell on the earth by [the means of] those miracles which he had power to do in the sight of the beast; saying to them that dwell on the earth, that they should make an image to the beast, which had the wound by a sword, and did live.

The false prophet tells the anti-Christ that he has designed a mark that will give them the power over all people. He reaches into the inner pocket of his suit and retrieves a paper showing a numerical figure totaling **666.** He tells him this number will govern 100% of everyone buying and selling, especially food products. The false prophet, smiling, tells him that is not all and reaches into another pocket and brings out a handful of agriculture seed with patented numbers on them. The anti-Christ returns the smile with instant understanding of the fusion of these two gifts. Satan, in the meantime, sits smiling, knowing that he has finally obtained the control of seed which will give more power to the mark than any other weapon.

Revelation 13:16 (KJV) And he causeth all, both small and great, rich and poor, free and bond, to receive a mark in their right hand, or in their foreheads: {to receive: Gr. to give them} 17 And that no man might buy or sell, save he that had the mark, or the name of the beast, or the number of his name.

Please understand, I am a simple man, a farmer with only a high-school education. The only thing I can say to you is, study the scriptures to gain wisdom and understanding. The previous two scriptures you read reminded me of the Bible verse that I started this book with, which is **Revelation 13:18.** It is the verse that I felt inspired to begin this book with. I hope it serves as a catalyst so that you search the scriptures to gain more wisdom and understanding. While you are searching the scriptures, I will not be offended if you do your best to prove this book, and me, wrong. I feel that I have written very little of this book and the Spirit has written most of it. I honestly feel we have just had a sneak preview into the conference room of hell.

16 THE PAINTING ON THE WALL

It's late in the year of 2006 and the Spirit of God is urging me to finish this book. The stages of writing have been laid out by the Master and I've simply had to furnish a weak fleshly body for the task. This weak body has fought with the Spirit and I failed many times and had to pull myself back up with the help of God.

Maybe I should rewrite the above paragraph and give credit where it is due. Not I, but God did it all. My pen has much more freedom now because of God having laid out certain circumstances in advance. Did He lay out the sins I've committed in my life? No! I willingly did that.

The trial that was suppose to take place in Huntsville Federal Court in late 2006 will not happen now. It will not happen because of certain happenings during hearings in court proceedings over the course of 2006.

The choice of not going to trial was made by me and me only. My enemy had no effect on my choice even though they will never believe what I just stated.

I know you would like for me to get to the point about the title of this chapter. The point is that in the Federal court room in Huntsville, Alabama, there is a painting on the wall behind where the Federal judge sits. There is also a writing on a plaque explaining the painting. There are several courtrooms in the Huntsville Federal courthouse. The courtroom with the painting is the courtroom where the hearings took place and my trial would have taken place.

The painting, the artist, and the writing on the plaque have a meaning my pen and I cannot write down with the power I wish I could. With God being my helpmate, I'll do my best. On

February 15, 1898 a man by the name of Xavier Gonzalez was born in Almeria, Spain. He immigrated to America from Spain in 1925 and became a naturalized citizen in 1931. He studied art at the Art Institute of Chicago, the San Carlos Academy in Mexico City, and the San Antonio Art School. In 1937 he painted a painting on the wall of the Federal Courtroom in Huntsville, Alabama. I had zero knowledge of this painting until April 2006. Even though my lawyers had seen this painting many times they had not told me of it.

As you walk into this courtroom, it immediately grabs your attention. During one hearing I noticed that one of Monsanto's lead lawyers made comments about it also. The painting is oil on canvas having the dimensions of 12 feet by 13 feet and 6 inches, covering most of the wall behind the judge.

I believe this to be the only courtroom in the world to have this painting on it. The first time I walked into this courtroom, my heart almost stopped when I saw it. After my first appearance in this courtroom in April of 2006, the painting would not leave my mind. I asked my first lawyer, Don Word of Scottsboro, if he had any thoughts pertaining to the meaning of the painting. He said it was a unique painting and he wasn't sure of what it meant. He had been in the courtroom in December 2005 for a hearing on my case, but I didn't go with him.

As you stand and look at this painting, the front and foremost visual part of the painting is a man standing bigger than life behind a stalk of corn. He's holding up two leaves of the stalk of corn, one on each side of the stalk. A stalk of corn usually has about ten leaves on it. The man in the painting is holding up leaves about mid-ways of the stalk.

The man with the stalk of corn is, without a doubt, the main focus of this giant painting. I make that statement because of the fact the people I observed talking about the painting, always mentioned the man and the corn first. My mind constantly had a visual picture of this painting as I tried to understand it for several months after having first seen it. The man holding the stalk of corn had to be the main theme because the artist placed him up front, larger than life.

In August 2003, I stood in a field and had a picture taken of me with a single stalk of corn. This picture was taken two and one-half years before I knew this courtroom painting existed. I have only been in this courtroom two times in my life as I pen down these words now. Both of my visits happened during 2006.

It's Sunday, December 3, 2006, as I sat in church writing these pages, my wife, Pam, rubs my thumb and hand as my hand tires from writing. My mind and the leading of the Spirit outruns the writing ability of my hand. This is actually a chapter that I wasn't expecting to write, and had it not been for the painting, I would not have written it. As I enter on into the writing of this chapter, you will see this chapter as being somewhat prophetic. Do not apply the word prophet to me because I do not match up with the requirements of a prophet, I fall dramatically short in that category. I do, however, believe the artist that painted the painting on the wall of the Federal courtroom was used in a prophetic manner.

During the Winter of 2005, and the Spring of 2006, my father, Wayne White, was dropped from the seed lawsuit. Monsanto agreed that they failed to provide any evidence my father had saved seed or misused their patents.

The hearing in April 2006 came as a surprise to me and my lawyers. We had a good feeling that the new judge I had acquired was going to change some of the ruling of the previous judge. Our good feeling, however, did not nullify the possibility that it could still be a bad experience for us. We had high hopes but at the same time were prepared for a let-down. My elderly father who with his health failing did not have to go to this hearing because his case had already been dismissed. I decided to take my father to the hearing even though I didn't have to. I explained to my father that he was out of the lawsuit and didn't have to go, but that I wanted him to.

My father's nerves could stand very little and he became emotionally upset when I asked him to go. I told him he didn't have to go but I wanted him to go. My fathers mental condition had gotten to the point that I could not make him understand, his lawsuit was over. He had great fear that Monsanto was going to sue him again. My attorneys were reluctant to allow him to go, but I just felt like I had to take him at least one time. My strategy for this was to let the brilliant, wealthy Monsanto lawyers at least have to look at the eighty-three year old man they had sued. The drive to Huntsville was physically painful to my father due to the broken hip he had received a few months before. Daddy never knew the reason I took him and I never told him.

As my father and I and my lawyers stood in the hall next to the courtroom with the U.S. Marshalls, an elevator door opened in front of us. Monsanto's lead lawyer, Joel Cape, and another lawyer stepped from the elevator door. I looked at Joel Cape's eyes as he unexpectantly saw my father. The expression on his face told the story I was expecting. He was shocked seeing my father there. I believe that was the last thing in the world he was expecting me to do. He simply stopped in his tracks and stared at my father, then me, then back at my father. He could shamelessly sue my elderly father from a high-rise office in New Orleans, but looking at my father in person left him speechless. He just wasn't prepared to look at the oldest man in the world that had ever been sued for saving seed since God created seed. I remember looking at Cape in a manner in which I have never looked at anyone. I was instructed by my lawyers to shake his hand, but to be truthful I wanted to ignore him, I shook his hand but it wasn't any fun.

Joel Cape is well aware of the mental torment their lawsuits places upon a farmer. He had tormented my father for almost three years. And in the duration of a second of time, the reality of what he had done to my father slammed his conscience. He looked at my father with just a blank stare and was barely able to shake his hand. My father was cleared of Monsanto's accusations, but Monsanto and Joel Cape still have to face God's judgement on the issue of suing Wayne White.

The lawyer with Cape who I believe to be from Birmingham, or Huntsville, Alabama, seemed to direct his initial shock towards Cape. I seemed to see sympathy in this Birmingham lawyer's eyes for my father. I really didn't consider this lawyer much of an enemy to me. I'll give him the grace of not mentioning his name. He did little, if anything, to help Cape during the hearing.

This was my first time in court and everything was new to me. I quickly settled in as my lead lawyer spoke brilliantly when he was given his allotted time. I was shocked at the aggressive attack and wisdom of my lead lawyer. Cape began to present his attack that I knew was crippled because of my father's presence. I noticed the lawyer that was suppose to help Cape was looking over at my father periodically. He sat several feet from Cape and had very little, if any, input.

As my lawyer presented his strongest points and actually seemed to be angry, I was thoroughly enjoying it. This was very comforting to me because I knew he could perform valiantly against Monsanto's professional. Cape stood up again and to me he seemed to be very confused. Little did he know a prayer chain of very godly people were praying for him to become confused at that very moment. These people had come to me and asked me what time the court started and told me they had been lead to pray confusion on Monsanto's lawyers. This was something Cape knew nothing of and could not do anything about if he had known it.

I got to see Cape's pants leg shake and also his paperwork was trembling. This Federal judge showed great wisdom. From all of my research I thought no one could handle Monsanto's lawyers. Maybe they just sent the wrong one that day because I think he fumbled the ball and accidentally kicked it and he tried to pick it up.

My lawyers brought up several issues that we had not mentioned prior to this court day. One of them was the defense of patent 605 and the invalidity against their patent number 605. We strongly felt that patent 605 was invalid and could be proved invalid before a jury. I believe Monsanto had great fear of that defense because if a jury found the patent invalid, they had no case against me and hundreds of other farmers.

After all, they were in Alabama where the chemical dumping in Anniston loomed over their head. They were before a brilliant judge who was capable of understanding the technical information about the patent. We felt the weakness of patent 605 was its written enablement. That simply means that the patent has to be written correctly to enable it to be valid. In patent 605 the word seed or saving seed is not even in the writing. Monsanto's patent 605 does have the word seed in it.

In the book, Monsanto Versus U.S. Farmers, written in 2005 by the "Center for Food Safety" are pictures of forged signatures by Monsanto representatives on Monsanto's technology agreements. The "Center for Food Safety" states the possibility of Monsanto having forged hundreds of farmers' signatures on their technology agreements. Also in the Monsanto Vs. U.S. Farmers book is the record of myself and my father names being listed as ongoing cases. According to the "Center for Food Safety" Monsanto filed 16 lawsuits in 2003. Four of those were against myself, my business, and my father.

During this hearing, I did not know for sure if I was allowed to speak, but planned to ask permission if a certain issue did not come up. That issue was the statement a licensed Monsanto seed salesman had made to me in the summer of 2003. This man's statement implied that a man in Tupelo, Mississippi, had already been killed as a result of one of these lawsuits. He also stated that he just wanted me to be aware of what I was into.

As we neared the end of this hearing, the Federal judge referenced me making a trip to Tupelo, Mississippi, in 2003. The judge wanted Monsanto to explain why I made that trip. Joel Cape, Monsanto's lead lawyer, called it a tragic situation and did not go into detail as completely as I wanted him to. However, that doesn't surprise me because I believe this situation was very damaging to Monsanto. Cape was having to deal with my father being in the courtroom and the possibility of one of their salesmen insinuating they killed a man in Mississippi and also made threats against me. Cape never seemed to recover after this portion of the hearing. I don't know if Cape knew what all the salesman said to me, but it was obvious that Cape did not want to say any more than he had to.

I believe this situation was hard on Monsanto. If they had fired him, they would be admitting guilt. If they didn't fire him, they knew we would certainly use it in the trial. If I had to pinpoint Monsanto's decision to choose mediation instead of trial, I would have to believe this scenario was the reason. Soon after these statements from Cape, the judge asked him if he wanted to mediate this case out, and Cape said he did. They had consistently demanded a jury trial up until this point.

The judge sent the case to mediation in the Birmingham, Alabama, Federal courthouse with a different Federal judge presiding. As we arrived in Birmingham my lawyers and I were somewhat surprised at who showed up with Monsanto's lawyers. It was none other than Scott Baucum, the man who I described in the first chapter of this book; the one who holds the job title, Manager Value Capture. For some reason, it did not shock me that he was there, although I had no knowledge of him ever assisting Monsanto's lawyers in the courtroom. In my mind, this man superseded all of Monsanto's lawyers and investigators in the power structure.

I actually counted it a blessing to face this man in a mind game and I depended on God to give me the words to say. I believe this man has a greater grip on seed than any other person in the world. I wasn't sure if Baucum knew about this book, but I had reason to believe he did. I believe he came with the soul purpose of silencing me and forcing me to become their puppet. If that was his motive, he failed to do so. I would love to tell you what all went on in mediation, but some parts are held confidential by the Federal court.

I would, however, challenge Monsanto or any of their officials, now or in the future, to a live debate unedited and uncensored on national television. Some of the discussions we had would be very interesting to you, the reader, but for now we can get by without them. I don't believe Baucum likes me very much and I doubt he will after this book comes out either. He will stand before God for his deeds in this life and I will stand before God for mine. And I don't want to swap places with him for the world. Enough said.

Mediation in Birmingham ended near midnight with me still wanting a jury trial and willing to go to one, although it would have exhausted me financially. In civil federal court, you can win with a jury and still lose when your opponents appeal. I believe Mitchell Scruggs of Tupelo, Mississippi, has spent at least five million dollars fighting Monsanto. Mr. Scruggs, in September 2006, suffered a severe setback in the United States Circuit of Appeals. If Mr. Scruggs loses his last appeal, Monsanto will demand millions of dollars of compensation. I was simply taking the same road Mr. Scruggs had paved and I would have run out of money before I reached the position Mr. Scruggs made it to.

I wish to thank Mr. Scruggs for bravely fighting Monsanto. He made a valiant effort to win back the farmer's right to save seed. Mr. Scruggs and his lawyers helped me greatly at no charge. He has stood in the gap for the farmers of the world in a manner which most people cannot imagine. I would like to thank his lawyers in giving my lawyers new ideas for defense which weakened Monsanto's case against me.

I titled this chapter, "The Painting on the Wall", and I'm just now getting to the meaning of that title. When my pen starts writing, it amazes me how the ink flows down words and sentences I haven't thought of. I give credit to God for directing my mind, my hand and my pen. Without my dependence on God this book could not be written. He has walked close with me during this very troubled time of my life and has not forsaken me.

It is hard for me to feel worthy enough to have His continued guidance. The next few pages will finish this chapter. The situation I'm about to write put me in the presence of God in a manner greater than I had ever imagined.

After making very little progress in the first mediation in Birmingham, I began to believe a trial was imminent. I was struggling for direction from God and wishing God had a cell phone. I then received a call from my lawyers and another mediation date had been set up by the judge from Birmingham. I asked my lawyers to see if we could have the mediation take place in Huntsville instead of Birmingham. I felt more comfortable in Huntsville because of the painting on the wall of the Huntsville Federal courtroom.

My lawyers were able to get the mediation held in Huntsville. When I received the call from my lawyers that the mediation would be held in Huntsville, it brought me peace of mind. For months now the painting on the wall was burned into my mind and I dwelled on it a lot. I had decided the man holding the stalk of corn in the painting and the 2003 picture of me holding the stalk of corn was more than a coincidence.

I remembered during the mediation in Birmingham I was wishing that I was in Huntsville because of the peace that the painting brought me. This new mediation date was actually a surprise to all of us because, when we left Birmingham, we thought we were headed to trial. The Birmingham judge just seemed, for some reason, to want to try one more time. He wasn't obligated to give us another mediation, but he chose to.

My not having a positive answer to the meaning of the painting was beginning to worry me. I knew it had the power to give me peace during the trial, but I still felt like there was something I couldn't put my finger on. I was confident, however, that the unknown mystery about the painting was spiritual and not carnal. This gave me confidence that I could leave Monsanto in darkness when I fully understood the painting. I believe they perceived it just as nice artwork, no more, no less. I honestly don't believe they ever made the connection of this seed trial being held in the only courtroom in the world with this agricultural mural painted on the wall.

This painting was now dominating my strategy and I was determined for this trial to end in the presence of this painting. During mediation I believe my attorneys began to recognize the importance of this painting to me. My attorneys had seen this painting many times and they became intrigued over my interest in it.

I knew Monsanto had the highest technology surveillance equipment available. There was one thing however that I had no fear of and that was Monsanto's ability to obtain intelligence of my discernment of what this painting meant. I knew Monsanto could not hack into God's purpose for this painting and what I was feeling. This was one of the first times I was one hundred percent certain I could leave Monsanto's lawyers totally in the dark. I knew I could do this legally and there was nothing Monsanto could do about it.

There was one thing that me and Monsanto shared in the presence of God, and that is the fact that I'm nothing and neither are they when it comes to God's wisdom.

The mediation process started around noon and continued into the night. Sometime during the late afternoon, I told the judge I wanted to go to the courtroom that the trial would take place in and look at the painting. Myself, My lawyers, and Monsanto's lawyers had been in a mental warfare for hours and agreements had been reached. I felt good about the agreements because they gave me the hope of peace which I had not had in over three years.

Sometime in the late evening, we found that the courtroom with the painting was locked and only the other judge had a key. This was a mental letdown for me because I knew the other judge was off duty. The deal that my lawyers had reached with Monsanto was okay with me except for the fact that I still had to see that painting one more time.

This was the second time mediation had went late into the night. There was also another farmer in the courtroom with his attorney and my attorneys. This other farmer had really suffered from Monsanto suing him. I was taking all the heat off of this farmer that I could. I felt sorry for this farmer because he was having severe financial difficulties. I intended to help him financially if he needed my help. He and his lawyers were letting me and my lawyers lead the strategy against Monsanto. Monsanto had not let up on this man for three years in their effort to make a poster boy out of me. I knew if it were not for me, Monsanto would not be pursuing this man.

I know that Monsanto lawyers and certain other people reading this book are hoping that I'll cross the line of confidentiality. Forget it. It's not going to happen, so sit down and read the rest of this chapter very slowly. I urge the Christians and whoever believes in this book to also read slowly and understand how God works.

It was getting late into the night now and Monsanto's lawyers, me, my lawyers, the other farmer, his lawyer, the judge and the U.S. marshals were the only people left in the courthouse. We were vastly approaching midnight and the time had come for me to sign the paperwork and end this court case or go to trial. Everyone knew all areas had been exhausted and everyone was focusing upon my decision. My lawyers had begged and pleaded and now even they were subdued. The other farmer and his lawyer had not put any pressure on me. I admired and appreciated them for letting me make the decision.

These next few paragraphs will lose Monsanto because they did not know what was happening at the time. They are only now about to find out what happened and I'm not sure they will understand it. They will probably have a hard time understanding it and I doubt they will ever believe it in its entirety.

I certainly had a brilliant team of lawyers with me that night, a fair judge, a good farmer friend and I felt he had an excellent lawyer. Even with all of these good men assisting me, I knew the time had come that it was just me and God.

I walked over to the corner of the courtroom and knelt down and silently prayed to God. My prayer was simple and plain. I prayed, "God, you know the point where I'm at in this process." I said, "God, if I can't see the painting, I have made my decision to go to trial which guarantees me the right to see the painting" I prayed, "God, I know the courtroom is locked and I hate to put you on the spot, but I've got to have a miracle. Please get me into the courtroom where I can look at that painting one more time before I make my final decision." I prayed, "God, I apologize for putting you on the spot and asking for an immediate answer." I prayed, "God, let me look at the painting and show me the meaning of it if I've been missing it." I prayed, "God, I know the man on the wall holding the stalk of corn strongly means something, so please let me see it. Amen." After I prayed that prayer silently I stood up and walked back toward the other farmer. He looked at me and told me he could tell from the look on my face that we were going to trial and I said, "Yes."

In a few minutes, the judge came over to me and said, "Michael, let's go up to the other courtroom and see the painting." I did not ask the judge if the courtroom was still locked because I felt he knew something he was not telling me. The other farmer, all of our lawyers and I went up to the other courtroom with the federal judge. For some reason, Monsanto's lawyer did not go with us and that suited me well although he could have if he had wanted to. I walked to the center of the courtroom and began to look over every scene in the painting. I remember the judge coming up beside me and asking me why Monsanto had never sued anyone for saving corn seed. I told him that if you save corn seed, the yield would be near zero. I believe I told him I had a picture of myself taken in 2004 standing behind a stalk of corn that volunteered in a field of soybeans. This stalk of corn was a genetically modified Monsanto round-up ready stalk. It should have put on approximately six- to eight-hundred kernels and it had only put on two very small rotten kernels.

I believe the judge told me he could tell this painting meant something to me. I have trouble remembering the exact words spoken over the next few minutes in that room. I openly asked everyone in the courtroom if they knew what this painting meant. About that time, my lead lawyer spoke up and said there was a plaque on the wall behind the judge's desk and it might contain an explanation about the painting.

My lawyer walked up into the judge's chamber and began to read the plaque. My lawyer began to read the plaque that someone had written about the artist who painted the painting in 1937. The plaque told of the artist moving to America. My lawyer then began describing the five figures in the painting.

The woman shouldering a basket of fruit symbolizes youth and fertility. The upper right hand-man pounding iron signifies work. The young man in the lower right-hand holds a corn stalk open as if it were a book. He represents scientific agriculture and the transition or learning from the environment to learning through the written source. My lawyer went on to read the rest of the plaque.

All of these explanations consumed about half of the plaque. I had begin to have fear that the man holding the stalk of corn would not be explained. The manner in which my lawyer was reading caused him to hesitate for a moment. And when my lawyer said the man holding up the two leaves of the corn stalk represents holding open the pages of a book I had become weak and actually thought I was going to pass out.

The word book, scientific agriculture, and written source sent my mind into a zone I have never been before. I had knowledge that this courthouse was going to be torn down soon and a new one built in Huntsville. About that time, one of the lawyers spoke up and said, "How did that man know to use the word *scientific agriculture* in 1937?" He said scientific agriculture did not even exist in 1937. Someone else spoke up and said it sounds like he was speaking prophetically. My lead lawyer turned around and smiled at me and stopped reading.

I was still shocked at the feeling I was feeling. It seemed like I could actually lift one of my hands and almost touch God. I quickly ran thoughts through my mind of the courtroom being torn down and this painting no longer existing. That meant if the artist's words were true, the book had to be written before the courtroom was torn down or about the same time it was torn down. About that time, I realized the book that I had written over a period of four years was the book the artist was talking about. Finally, I understood the meaning of the man holding the stalk of corn. And I turned to my lawyers and peacefully said, "I'll sign the papers now."

The window of opportunity for the book to come out was at hand. If I went on to trial, I would not be allowed to put the book out for several more years if ever. I felt I had to take the window of opportunity that God had given me. Missing that window would cause the painting to lose its spiritual validity. God had this artist paint this painting seventy years prior to this book being completed. Seventy is God's perfect number.

I hold no right to claim any ability to say I have been used prophetically. I can, however, with liberty state that the vessel I walk in helped the artist become a prophet. I do not believe I will ever be allowed on this earth to experience the feeling that I felt that night. It was a factual feeling presented right in front of me. The painting on the cover of this book is the actual mural from the courtroom. This mural helps to authenticate this book and its title, "The 666's Are in the Seed" in a manner in which I could have never dreamed of.

I can honestly state that if the word "book" was not on that plaque you might not be reading this book. I can also say without the existence of my picture of a corn stalk and the man in the painting and his corn stalk, you might not be reading this book. Without these important events I would have most likely went to trial. Somewhere during the process of the four year battle I transcended to wanting to defeat Monsanto and let the book take second place.

Monsanto has very deep pockets and civil court and all the appeals that would have followed probably would have destroyed me financially and emotionally. The painting on the wall and the words written on the plaque place me back on the right way, God wanted me on. God will deal with Monsanto in due season and he is much more qualified and powerful than I am.

Monsanto, as much as we are enemies, I still have to pray for you and your lawyers. I can't apologize for you not being in the room with us that night. I guess God just didn't allow you to be in there.

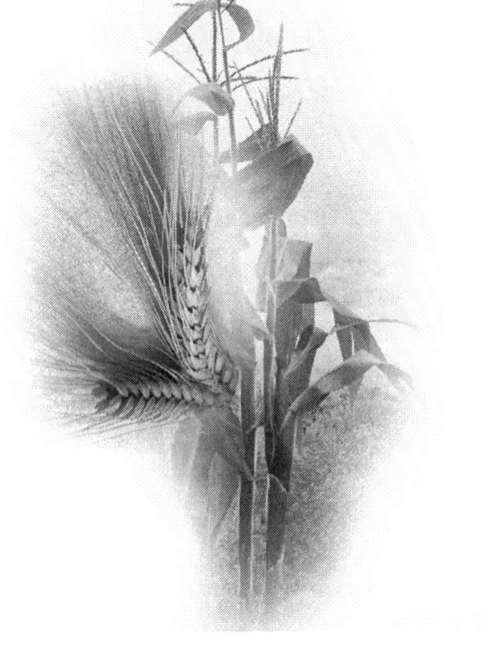

17 Seeing the End

The writing I'll do today may be of a different kind. It seems I feel beaten down in mind and spirit. My battles are too many and too heavy at times and I want to quit, but I can't. I'm proud that Monsanto doesn't know when I'm this weak, they would know when to attack and finish me off. However, by the time they read this battlefield secret, I hope to be on a mountain and their shooting will fall short. I can feel and hear hoof beats of horses bringing injustice toward this troubled world. Those horses causing the hoof beats that I hear have corporate, political, and heathen immoral riders. The largest horses have spiritual wickedness riding on them. In their hands they have room for deceitful wickedness to attack what is left of morality and Christians of this world. The reigns that are going to these horses mouths have no reason to occupy the hand of the rider, for these horses know where they are going, because it's allowed in God's plan.

Revelation 6:1 (KJV) And I saw when the Lamb opened one of the seals, and I heard, as it were the noise of thunder, one of the four beasts saying, Come and see.

2 And I saw, and behold a white horse: and he that sat on him had a bow; and a crown was given unto him: and he went forth conquering, and to conquer.

3 And when he had opened the second seal, I heard the second beast say, Come and see.

4 And there went out another horse [that was] red: and [power] was given to him that sat thereon to take peace from the earth, and that they should kill one another: and there was given unto him a great sword.

5 And when he had opened the third seal, I heard the third beast say, Come and see. And I beheld, and lo ***a black horse****; and he that sat on him had* ***a pair of balances in his hand.***

6 And I heard a voice in the midst of the four beasts say, A measure of wheat for a penny, and three measures of barley for a penny; and [see] thou hurt not the oil and the wine. {A measure: the word choenix signifieth a measure containing one wine quart, and the twelfth part of a quart}

7 And when he had opened the fourth seal, I heard the voice of the fourth beast say, Come and see.

8 And I looked, and behold a pale horse: and his name that sat on him was Death, and Hell followed with him. And power was given unto them over the fourth part of the earth, to kill with sword, and with hunger, and with death, and with the beasts of the earth. {unto them: or, to him}

I'm in the path of some of those horses trying to write this book. I don't mean to cry on anyone's shoulder. I accept this battle . . . believing God will sustain me and this book will serve its purpose.

I took my two daughters to a steakhouse last night and watched people go to the bountiful buffet lines as many times as they wanted. For ten dollars there was no limit as to how much food a person could eat. Also, you didn't have to show a mark on your forehead or hand to purchase this food. These horses that I spoke of are coming to govern and control such eating places as the steakhouse we ate at. Are they going to ride their horse up in the parking lot and lock the door? No, Revelation 6:5 tells of the rider of a black horse, with a pair of balances in his hand. John, the revelator, saw the person sitting on the black horse in detail;

he also heard a voice speak in the midst of these horses telling the purpose of this black horse. Looking at the main focus of this very important horse, we understand its sole purpose is to bring a pair of balances to earth. Balances represent scales that weigh with pinpoint accuracy. In our courtrooms and government buildings there are images of balances presented to represent the scales of justice.

Scales are designed to weigh any and all type of matter in existence today. I believe you would be hard pressed to find any food eaten that is not sold by weight and measurements. I believe the balances in Revelation 6:5 represent food and justice measurements. Remember, there are two types of justice . . . injustice and justice. This horse, without a doubt, carries balances that weigh out injustice. Any true Christian is hearing this horse coming. Surely this black horse now says, and will say, that he provides American and World justice. However, the rider is a liar and master of deceit. So recognize his hoof beats for what they are.

I see in the empty hands of the horse's rider many systems that will be in place when the horses get here. They are carrying the keys to the systems that have already been built and are being built. Also, these balances represent the weighing and control of food. John the revelator saw this vision with God-given accuracy. He saw the balances weighing out wheat and barley in Revelation 6:6. Both wheat and barley are grains that have a dual purpose, they can be used to feed both humans and animals. Humans can grow and process the two grains very easily. You can pick up two stones and grind them together to process these grains and turn them into bread. You can also plant these grains to graze cattle, sheep, and many other meat animals. We're now getting to the heart and core make-up of this book. This horse is next in line behind the white and red horse described in Revelation chapter 6. This horse, no doubt, has a very important purpose, as do all of the others. What is its purpose? No doubt, it is symbolic for the control of food. The horse that follows him, the pale horse, has the power to control death with a sword and hunger. John saw the pale horse having the power to kill 25 percent of the world's population. The scripture does not say what percent of the 25 percent is killed with hunger or what percent is killed with the sword. I guarantee you hunger causes soldiers and the general population to become easy prey for the sword. I believe I can say with the power of the Spirit that hunger will kill a higher percentage or have a final result of being dominant as to killing a higher percentage of people in the pale horse's death count.

Let's go back to the black horse. The black horse will make the pale horse's job easier. There is no doubt patented seed can be controlled. Read some of the lawsuits of the farmers that are being sued for saving seed, or talk to some of the farmers themselves and you will see what I mean. Suffer a Monsanto lawsuit, or try to farm without being caught or threatened by a seed patent and true understanding will take control over your mind. According to Monsanto, farmers must control pollen flow. We've got to "control the wind" and many other things right now to farm without having any patented plants to spring up among millions in your field. I do not think there is a farm of any size in the U.S. anymore that does not have some patented seed growing either known or unknown in its fields. This contamination of patented genetically modified seed has occurred even without the introduction of the Terminator Gene on a large scale yet.

I believe the balances carried by the rider of the black horse have a deeper meaning than I have previously known. I feel I must ask God to help me with this statement so that it is penned in a manner in which God wants it penned. I believe these balances represent the weighing of seed, patented or unpatented, all of which will require the mark to purchase. I believe they also represent the weighing of seed that has not been affected by the

Terminator Gene during the great tribulation. John saw wheat, not flour. I believe that if he saw food being weighed on these balances he would have said flour and wheat, two different things. In chapter 18 of Revelation, John saw wheat and flour being two different items.

Revelation 18:10 (KJV) Standing afar off for the fear of her torment, saying, Alas, alas, that great city Babylon, that mighty city! for in one hour is thy judgment come. 11 And the merchants of the earth shall weep and mourn over her; for no man buyeth their merchandise any more: 12 The merchandise of gold, and silver, and precious stones, and of pearls, and fine linen, and purple, and silk, and scarlet, and all thyine wood, and all manner vessels of ivory, and all manner vessels of most precious wood, and of brass, and iron, and marble, {thyine: or, sweet} 13 And cinnamon, and odors, and ointments, and frankincense, and wine, and oil, and ***fine flour, and wheat****, and beasts, and sheep, and horses, and chariots, and slaves, and souls of men. {slaves: or, bodies}.*

Wheat seed with good germination is priceless when compared to wheat seed with no germination. Please understand that wheat and wheat seed are the same. When wheat is processed into flour, it is ready to become a food item, or bread. When wheat is planted in the soil, it is then counted as seed. Then this wheat that has been planted begins its growth toward a wheat stalk maturing into dozens of kernels of wheat. The end result of that wheat's stalks fruit gives us the definition of seed having seed in itself. It is possible to take a bushel of wheat (60 pounds) in U.S. standard and produce 50 bushels of wheat by planting it and taking proper care of it. It is then possible to take that one bushel that you planted to harvest 3,000 pounds of wheat. One bushel of wheat will make 60 loaves of bread. Plant that bushel of wheat and you could end up with 3000 loaves of bread instead.

A measure of wheat in Revelation is 12 pounds. That would make 12 loaves of bread. Plant that 12 pounds of wheat and you can have 600 loaves of bread as an end result.

It is now September 2007 and I've spent over four years writing this book. I have made many changes and corrections as the situations have changed. In the past few days, wheat has hit record prices of nine dollars plus. Farmers, knowing that I am no longer in the seed business, have approached me asking me to find them wheat seed. I made several phone calls and wheat seed is very scarce and high priced. I'm actually having to drive out of state to pick up a hundred bags of wheat seed. Less than three years ago, I could have found thousands almost anywhere I inquired. I have still not been able to locate any barley seed whatsoever.

I would like to inform you that if America plants a less than normal wheat crop this year, due to a wheat seed shortage, it could be avoided because of the wheat in storage. The problem with the wheat in storage is that it contains patented genes. If it was removed from the storage facility then planted, it would produce almost the same result as the high priced wheat seed in bags. The problem is that if a farmer retrieves patented wheat from his storage bins, he stands a good chance of facing a patent infringement lawsuit. There is ample wheat in storage facilities to plant an abundant crop in 2007, but the patent laws on second generation seed will prevent this stored wheat from being used for seed.

Hoof prints of the powerful black horse are already being made upon America's farmland and dinner table. With wheat soaring to nine dollars, bread prices have no choice but to increase. With the increase of food prices, more and more people are unable to afford food. The black horse's purpose is already being felt.

I would like to use some of Joel Cape's speech from

the "Southeast Farm Press" of March 8, 2006. Remember Joel Cape is the Monsanto lawyer who was my opponent in the Federal courtroom. He states that:

> In 1839, the commissioner of patents, Henry Ellsworth, secured funding from Congress to collect and distribute agricultural seed and statistics. That, in turn, established a free seed distribution program through the Postal Service. Besides letters, seed was sent through the Postal Service five years prior to any other parcel being sent.
>
> **Fairly successful**
>
> The program was fairly successful, said Cape. Ten years after it started, the Patent Office sent out 60,000 packages of seed annually. By 1855, the office had shipped out over 1 million seed packages.
>
> Another paragraph reads:
>
> The USDA's program was far and away the most successful. "About 15 years after it was established, about a third of the entire USDA budget was devoted to the free seed distribution program. By the turn of the century, USDA was sending out 22 million packages of seed yearly. Each of those packages contained five packets of seed. So, essentially, by 1900, they were sending out over 1 billion packages of seed."

I appreciate Mr. Cape providing me this information that I did not know. I would like to profile the fact that 107 years ago the USDA was giving away 1 billion packages of free seed. We have progressed so much in those 107 years that if I gave away or sold one small pack of Monsanto's free seed, Cape and Monsanto could sue me and cost me hundreds of thousands of dollars. Mr. Cape, have you ever rode a black horse? Maybe you're riding one now and do not even know it. Mr. Cape, one other thing, I would love to debate you live on national television.

I've faced evil charges of seed patent infringement in this pre-rapture trial. After the rapture, if someone saves and plants patented seed, or un-patented seed, without the mark on their right hand or forehead, they will face the punishment of death, or at least be forced into an unpleasant lifestyle. If people saving seed now suffer as my family has, just try to imagine post-rapture. John said, in Revelation 6:6, a measure of wheat for a **penny**. A penny is a Greek word meaning denarion in the New Testament. A denarion is a gold coin worth 25 silver coins. Twelve pounds of wheat for a very valuable gold coin. In today's terms that would be equal to trading 12 loaves of bread for several hundred dollars. Food is the most precious item to sustain daily human life. As I have said before, no seed, no food.

Most people only purchase food. Less than 1 and ½ percent of today's U.S. population are farmers. I believe 95 percent of those farmers have signed onto the seed agreement with Monsanto and other large corporations. That leaves 50 out of 1,000 people right now not signed into these binding agreements. I would not rule out the possibility that the figure could even be closer to 98 percent compliance. These agreements are here to stay, they will not leave with the rapture. The only thing I can see changing in them is the severity of the penalty. Information on farmers is now sufficient for the anti-Christ to have no problems if he stepped into power today. Farmers who go in the rapture will have their farms taken over and run by World Government appointed workers or those farms will be taken out of production. Enough food will be produced to feed the military, government employees of important stature, and other select few. All of those people will have to get prepared to take the mark in order to keep their status and purchase food. I can now see farmers being among the very first people to be required to take the mark. Many strenuous conditions will accompany a farmer taking the mark and buying seed. Because of my litigation with Monsanto, it is illegal for me to possess, buy, sell, or give away a single Monsanto genetically modified seed, according to Monsanto's laws. Anyone who wishes to leave the system after the rapture will suffer death or threats from persecution of themselves, family and friends. The mark will be available and required for all humans.

The black horse introduces severe food shortages; it does not cause a shortage of the mark of the beast. It actually enhances the mark because food shortage is now a fact, instead of a prophesy or prediction. As people grow more hungry, they will come to receive the mark. Hunger will make good men kill to feed their families. They will also give their soul to the mark to feed their families. I do not believe a man or woman who is in charge of their household will be able to buy and bring back food to their families, even if they receive the mark. I believe every member of the household, including children, will have to have the mark to partake of food purchased with the mark. There will be no justice and you will have no right to file a lawsuit. If you even suggest such a statement, you will be silenced. Almost all farmers who have been in litigation with Monsanto have already been silenced. Absolutely no gardens will be allowed, there is no seed anyway. If anyone has seed saved when the rapture takes place, it will become illegal, also germination drops unless kept in a freezer, but no mark . . . no electricity to run the freezer. Also, I believe it is possible that the terminator gene will have already taken its toll on all seed. I believe the terminator gene jumps species and has the capability to affect many seed-bearing organisms. God gave us seed to turn into food and Monsanto is helping install a plan for the anti-Christ to take seed and food away. The 666's are in the seed even as I speak.

I realize that many will say I'm crazy. I expect and understand some people thinking that. I'm human and I've had to pray and question myself. I believe I had to experience this very troubled time in my life to write this book. When I began writing it, I was scared at what I was writing down. Now, I'm searching for the most dangerous of the anti-Christ and end-time secrets to put down on the pages of this book. Every secret revealed means souls saved before the rapture. Unsaved reader, its altar call again. If you missed the first one, don't miss this one. Give your life to Christ before you die or the rapture takes place. Either one of these two events can take place in your life at any moment. Do not go through the mental agony and persecution of the anti-Christ. Do not take any more chances of dying and going to hell. If the convicting Spirit of God is speaking to you in your heart, don't turn Him away. My body, mind, nerves, courage, sanity, and pen have almost finished this task to endure and write this book. The food shortages have begun. The honey bees are almost gone. The Terminator Gene with its altered fertility is being approved and planted. Our government has recently approved animal cloning. In the fall of 2007, many farmers could not find wheat seed to plant. It is now spring of 2008 and farmers are begging for soybean seed and having little or no success in finding them.

I pray something in this book causes conviction upon your soul and enlightens your heart and you give your heart to GOD. I suffer Monsanto's retaliation willfully for your revelation and to enlighten you of the actual alignment of the evil end. Evil for those who miss the rapture, and eternal heavenly blessings for those who die in Christ or go in the rapture. The anti-Christ, Satan, and Monsanto will only do what God allows them to do to me. I'm suffering and hurting in this temporary life, but I am thankful to have been given the chance to help expose what I believe, to be one of, the greatest secrets in existence today. End-time puppets of the anti-Christ, I'm glad to leave you knowing that the world has an open door to look in and see the hand-written message upon the wall of a room, that has a door you cannot close On this wall is written, ***"The 666's are in the seed**."*

The Author's Summary

The demons have raged in laughter as they screamed for endurance. That endurance they wish for is unattainable in their limited power, giving way to the supreme God. I now taunt them as Elijah did the prophets of Baal. I have fought their best and with God's armor have received their darts and spears only as the air being pierced by nothing of nothings. I, with God's guidance, have run the race that few men imagine and of those that do imagine, most run away from and not toward.

I have heard from the God of Daniel and before Him I have numbered my sins as the number of the commandments. I am vain in His holy presence and ashamed of my work, for I am a man, which is flesh. Never the less, I must gather myself to do battle with the son of perdition. It has been my destiny. This battle is a battle of choice and I know the heat is fierce, because he is of fierce countenance.

I choose to lay in silence until the war is pledged by my adversary. Then will I emerge from the womb to the center of the battle, therefore being behind my enemy while he anticipates a forward attack. I see God's face and it is a mirror and in it I see my childlike vanity.

—Michael W. White

My father and mother were in this condition when Monsanto sued him. This picture was taken days after I told him of the lawsuit. My mother passed away a few months after the suit was filed.

A stalk of Monsanto's genetically modified corn that volunteered from the ground in 2004. This stalk is equal to a saved seed, it withered in the field. (Joel 1:17)

Myself standing with the stalk of corn that I used to explain Joel 1:17 with. This picture was taken 2 years before I knew the courtroom painting existed.

The largest grain storage facility in Jackson County, Alabama being torn down. (2005) The barns are broken down. (Joel 1:17)

Myself, holding a hand operated grain harvesting tool used in Joel's day to garner in the grain. Also, in the background, a modern day grain harvesting machine (Combine). The garner's are laid desolate. (Joel 1:17)

Myself in the Federal courtroom in Huntsville, Alabama where formal litigation took place. The mural on the wall inspired "The Painting On the Wall" chapter.

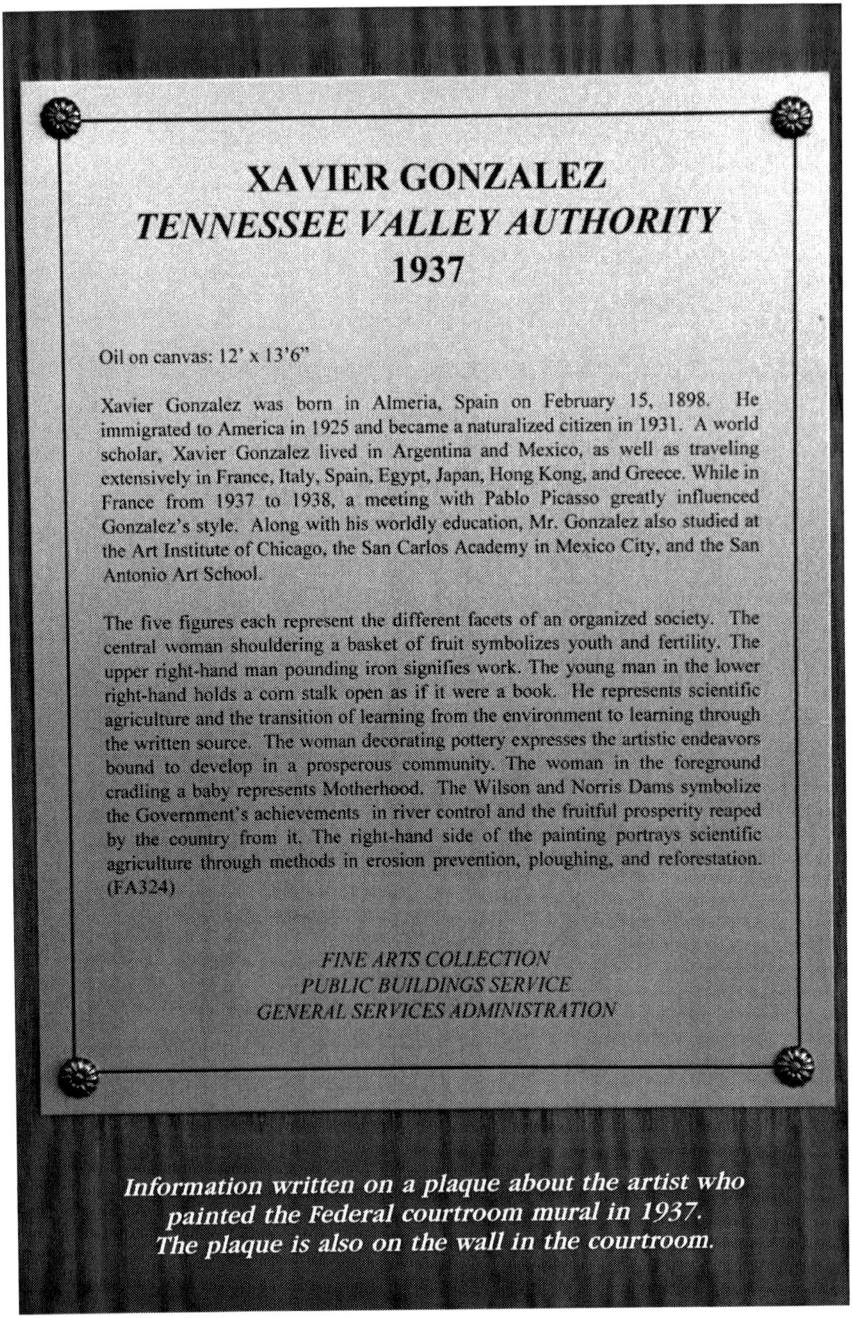

Information written on a plaque about the artist who painted the Federal courtroom mural in 1937. The plaque is also on the wall in the courtroom.